Marriage

What makes a marriage of two decades begin to unravel? There are no simple answers.

Alex and Miriam met-cute at the famous Strand bookstore in Manhattan. It was love at first sight for both of them. Their marriage was blissful. They had a son. All wonderful.

But in every family there are secrets and lies, and theirs was no different.

An unloving father, The suicide of a beloved sibling. A hidden diary, revealing more secrets, An unknown sibling. A son who is gay and wants nothing more than to be on the stage. An unrewarding job. A lousy boss. A sexual predator. Suddenly a life going nowhere.

But there is something more. Alex is on a quest, not just for knowledge and truth. He wants desperately to be a good husband, a good father, a good son. He doesn't know if he can achieve this but he knows he must try.

ACKNOWLEDGMENTS

It's been one hell of a ride. I began writing this novel more than a decade ago. Don't ask me why I didn't give up on it because I have no idea. I don't even remember what inspired me to begin writing it in the first place. At the time I was a member of the Ashawagh Hall Writer's Workshop. It was the brainchild of Marijane Meaker, the prolific Young Adult writer. She ran it for thirty years and was succeeded by Laura Stein, who has unfortunately passed away.

We met once a week. Three writers would bring ten pages, maximum, double spaced. Everyone received them in advance, so the comments were both written on the script as well as spoken in class.

When I knew my turn was scheduled, I would work doubly hard to make sure I had the best version I could come up with. No matter. There were usually plenty of suggestions as to how to make it better.

The criticism of this group was what kept me going, year after year. I finished one version and began another and just kept going. Marijane, Laura, and others, such as Lynn Blue, Rob Stuart, Ed Hannibal, and so many others, all deserve recognition for their astute comments.

In addition, I owe a lot to my family: children, grandchildren, nieces, nephews, and of course, to my love, Estelle.

Thank you and thank you.

OTHER BOOKS BY ROBERT BORIS RISKIN

The Jake Wanderman Mystery series
Scrambled Eggs
Deadly Bones
Deadly Secrets

www.robertborisriskin.com
Like me on Facebook

SHADOWS

Robert Boris Riskin

A Black Opal Books Publication

GENRE: MYSTERY/FAMILY DRAMA

First Publication: JUNE 2022

Published by Black Opal Books **http://www.blackopalbooks.com**

The great mystery is not that we should have been thrown down here at random between the profusion of matter and that of the stars; it is that from our very prison we should draw, from our own selves, images powerful enough to deny our nothingness.
Andre Malraux, Man's Fate

The fathers have eaten a sour grape, and the children's teeth are set on edge.
Isaiah—31:29

August 1949

The rock had originally been in a plastic box obtained from an art supply store. She had mounted it on a piece of foam core and had typed its description on a 3x5 index card that she then taped to the top of the box. It was her proudest possession, always kept on the table next to her bed.

Clarice had checked into the Holiday Inn in Boston without any luggage. She had brought her rock with her. They found it placed carefully in the middle of the bed as if it were on display.

"It's a piece of a meteor," she had told him when he was little and he had, of course, believed her. She was his older sister. She knew everything and explained everything. "I found it once on a night when the moon was full. I wasn't searching for it, how could I? I was just looking up at the heavens. And suddenly, there it was, at the foot of a tree, gleaming, shimmering, like a star. Actually, I like to think it found me."

She had not taken off her coat when she went over to the window. She still had it on when she pushed the window open, stepped out, and went down fourteen stories.

He had just graduated from college and was working at the summer camp he'd gone to as a child when he heard what had happened. His parents were too overwrought to do the formal identification. He agreed to make the trip.

The medical examiner had warned him it would be difficult. It was worse than difficult, worse than anything he could have imagined. There was a stench in the morgue that made him gag. When they drew back the sheet that covered her he felt his lips twisting in an attempt to keep from vomiting. Tears ran in a hot stream down his cheeks. Strangely, her face showed only a few bruises. With her eyes closed, he saw once again the extraordinary length of her lashes and remembered how fierce and dark her eyes were when she would tell him about the stars and how one could read the future in them. As he continued to look at her, she began to seem unreal, and he felt himself entering into some kind of transcendent state where he and his sister were together floating like astronauts in the darkness of outer space.

Later, he had listened to the speculation of others as to the meaning of what she had left on the bed in that hotel room, a riddle none of them had been able to solve. But he was quite sure he knew the answer to the riddle. It was that not even a part of a "heavenly body" had been enough to overcome what had been done to her. Even her beloved stars had failed her in the end.

Chapter 1
October 1975

His father died on a Friday. While his father had been anything but observant, Alex insisted that his mother follow Jewish tradition, having the funeral take place as quickly as possible, in this case a Sunday, the first day after the Sabbath. His mother had wanted no official mourning period, but Alex stayed home from work for three days. Even though he didn't give a shit about his father he wanted his boss and the people who worked under him to know that he was a Jew and that he observed Jewish customs. He was the executive assistant to the boss of a factory that produced silver-plated hollowware, bowls, cups, and candelabra. "Executive Assistant" was a fancy name for his job, which consisted of doing everything to run the factory but the selling. That was his boss's job. Most of the factory workers were Latinos and probably Catholic. He thought they might lose respect for him if he came back to work right away.

The following Sunday, exactly a week after the funeral, Alex got a call from his mother saying she wanted him to come over to her house.

"Now?"

"If you've got the time."

"Sure. I can do it. What's this about?

"I'll tell you when you get here," she said.

His wife, Miriam, was at the kitchen table with the Sunday Times spread out in front of her.

"Anything interesting happening?" he asked.

"New York City is just about bankrupt. Abe Beame is trying to get the feds to help."

"Good luck with that. Not with President Ford in charge."

"Who was on the phone?"

"My mother. She wants me to come over," he said.

"So?" She didn't look up.

"I don't know when I'll be back."

"Doesn't matter," she said, still not looking up.

It did not surprise him that she continued reading the newspaper. It did not surprise him that she seemed to be enveloped in a chilled vapor, that her words were suspended in the air as if they were icicles. "See you later, then," he said.

He walked out to the car feeling the tiny circle of pain in his chest. It was about the size of a dime, located just above the solar plexus. It had arrived one day without warning. He wasn't sure when, but it was a long time ago so he knew it had nothing to do with his father. He'd just finished brushing his teeth and was rinsing the toothbrush when he first became aware of it. He'd thought it was indigestion so he chewed a couple of Tums. But the dull pain didn't go away. It took a while before he came to the conclusion that it must have to do with what had been happening between him and Miriam. Their marriage, which he had always thought solid and enduring, had gradually changed, leaving behind this residue of persistent pain. He recognized it was similar to the ache he'd felt for at least a year after Clarice died.

He drove to his mother's house in Valley Stream, to the block with its narrow lawns and its neat little Cape Cods on fifty by a hundred lots. Everyone in this neighborhood made a living with his hands. His father, a tool and die man, had been considered top dog, the bluest of the blue collars.

He still had a key to the house but rang the bell. He could hear the familiar *dong-ding-dong*, and then his mother opened the door and turned her head with the trim brown pageboy to the side so he could kiss her cheek.

She had kept her figure, and colored her hair. She wore mourning black, but nevertheless looked chic. Gold dangled in circles from her ears, a necklace lay in an intricate pattern on her chest. He did not recall having seen that jewelry before.

He followed her into the kitchen and at a gesture from her, sat at the Formica table. Everything was the same as it had always been: the hard chairs, the round clock on the wall, the pale-yellow walls. He had grown up in this house; there wasn't a room that didn't have an echo.

There was a kettle on the stove, the water gurgling, the spout sending out puffs of steam, and the beginning of an eardrum hurting whistle. His mother lifted the kettle, changing the scream to a wail, and poured boiling water into pink and green flowered mugs already on the table, a tea bag in each one.

"Two tea bags?" he asked. "You always used to use one for two cups."

"Your father insisted on it. Now I use whatever I want."

"What about electricity?" His voice changed, in mock imitation of his father: "You left the lights on again. Is your name The Electric Company?"

His mother did not smile. "Old habits are hard to break."

There was a bowl of sugar on the table, another with packets of Sweet N' Low, and a plate of oatmeal cookies which he knew had come out of a box. His mother had never baked and had made no secret of her desire to spend as little time in the kitchen as possible. He could rarely remember the smell of cooking in the house. What remained in his memory was coming home from school—father at work, Clarice off on one of her shoplifting expeditions, mother out, and that empty feeling on finding the expected note. *Dad says to clean up the yard. Will be home for dinner. Mother.*

She put the kettle back on the stove. "Do you want milk? I know you sometimes take milk in your tea." When he shook his head, she sat opposite him.

He took the teabag out of the mug, put it on his napkin, and stirred in a teaspoon of sugar. He sipped carefully. His father used to put in three spoons of sugar, then drink it down like water. "How are you doing?" he asked.

"As well as can be expected."

"That's good."

This was how it had always been with his mother, always a strategic distance between them. She had called him for a reason, but he knew not to ask for the reason. He would wait for her to tell him.

His mother put her cup down and looked at him as if she were studying his face. "You don't look well. You're flushed. Do you have a fever?"

"No," he said. "I'm okay."

"I could always tell when you were getting sick," she said. "Not that you got sick that often."

Before he could restrain himself, he said, "You could always tell? I guess that's when I was really little. I don't remember you being around much to tell anything about me."

"That's not in the least true. I paid a lot of attention to you. Didn't I always go to open school nights?"

"What was I thinking? Of course. Forgive me."

"I don't like it when you're sarcastic."

He realized he was angry and upset about Miriam and

taking it out on his mother. "I'm sorry. I didn't mean that."

"I know how you felt about your father but I didn't think you thought so little of me. I've always loved you. Maybe I didn't give you as much attention as I gave Clarice, but now that you're an adult I'm sure you can understand why. She needed so much."

He put his cup down. "I said I'm sorry. And I don't want to talk about Clarice."

She nodded. "That's not what I called you for, anyhow."

"Okay, why did you call?" Finally, he thought. The talk about love had unsettled him. He couldn't remember the last time he'd heard the word escape his mother's lips.

She said, "It's only one little notebook."

"What is? I'm not following you."

"I was cleaning out the basement. It was under his workbench. It wasn't hidden. Maybe he wanted me to find it."

"What are you talking about?"

"I found a cookie tin in the basement. You know, the kind those imported cookies come in? The ones they sell in the supermarket? I used to get them on sale. It had letters in it."

"Whose letters?"

"All the letters you and your sister ever wrote home, or most of them anyway. There weren't that many. Mostly they were from when you went away to camp. And the ones Clarice wrote from that looney bin. And a couple you wrote from college…a letter I wrote him before we were married."

"He saved all those?"

"Can you believe it?" she said. "I had no idea. He never breathed a word of it." She paused. "There was something else there, too. There was a diary. Under the cookie tin."

He laughed. "A diary? From that old bastard Max

Gunther? I don't believe it. Are you sure it's his?"

His mother had made a face when he'd said "old bas-tard," but all she said was, "It's his, all right.

"It's hard to believe he kept a diary." Alex bit into a cookie.

"Are you hungry?" his mother asked. "I could fix you something."

He wasn't the least bit hungry and the thought of what she might offer him did not increase his appetite. "No. This is fine." He sipped the tea. "So I assume you read every-thing, including the diary."

"Yes."

"And? What was in it?"

She paused. "I don't think I ought to tell you. I think you should read it. I want you to read it yourself."

"You don't want to tell me anything?"

She shrugged, put both hands on the edge of the table, and stood up. "I'll get it."

☙❧

He remembered that in music class he'd chosen the clarinet. He'd taken a liking to the playing of Artie Shaw. At first he practiced in the living room. His father sat in the wing chair with Clarice on his lap. Clarice was twelve but big for her age. She looked uncomfortable. His mother sat on the couch reading the newspaper.

"What is that?" his father asked. His fingers played with Clarice's hair as he looked over at Alex.

"Scales," Alex said.

"I don't know much about music, but I know that's not music."

"I have to learn the notes first."

"He has to practice," his mother said, without looking up from the paper. "Everyone who wants to play an instrument has to practice."

"It hurts my ears. Clary's too. Don't it hurt your ears, Clary?"

Clarice squirmed but didn't say anything.

"I can tell you're never going to be much good at it. Why don't you try writing poetry, like Clarice? Might suit you better. At least we won't have to listen to you practice. Right, Clary?" And he laughed and bent to nuzzle Clarice's neck.

Clarice jumped off her father's lap. "Why don't you leave him alone?"

"Did you say something, missy? Are you talking to me?"

Clarice ran out of the room and up the stairs.

"I'll deal with you later," his father shouted after her. "I'll be up there to talk to you later. You can count on it!"

His words were as sharp and ruthless as a paper cut.

He saw his mother look at his father for a moment, then went back to reading her newspaper.

⌒⌒⌒

His mother returned. She was holding the metal cookie box and on top of it was a school notebook, the black and white kind with a white rectangle on the cover where you could write in the name of a subject. She placed the items carefully on the table as if they were fragile enough to break and stood with her hands at her sides.

He stared at the notebook, then reached out and placed one hand flat on the cover, fingers spread wide. He had long fingers. The music teacher had said he had the hands of a pianist. He didn't tell her his father thought music was a waste of time. His father used to say to him, "Music is for girls, or maybe you'd like to be a ballet dancer? You could become a full-time sissy." He felt the hardcover of the notebook under his fingers. The urge to open it was strong, but something held him back. He moved his hand away and stared at the notebook as if he were trying to read it through the cover.

"Aren't you going to open it?" his mother asked.

"Sure. Sure I'm going to open it. What about the box with the letters?"

"Why don't you just take this for now? You can go through those another time."

His breathing had become shallow. He took a deep breath, not looking at his mother, but aware of her eyes on him.

"What's the matter?" his mother asked.

"Nothing."

"Are you afraid? You think it's going to hurt you?"

"Will it?"

"You'll have to read it to find out."

Her eyes met his, locked briefly with a message he couldn't decipher, then slipped away.

He picked up the notebook and opened the cover. The first page was blank. The blankness leaped up at him. He had expected to find something written there: his father's name, or a date, something to show what it was, who it belonged to. He turned the page and saw his father's handwriting, the letters small, slanted backward. He saw words but couldn't absorb their meaning. He felt his mother watching him, and snapped the book shut.

"What's the matter?" she asked again.

"I don't want to read it now."

"Why not?"

"Not with you standing there watching me."

"When I realized the notebook was a diary my stomach did flip flops," she said. "Your father keeping a diary? I couldn't believe it. And you know what? I didn't read it at first, either. As a matter of fact, I almost threw it in the garbage. But then I thought, what if it proves you're all wrong about him? That he never did any of those things you accused him of?"

"And did it?"

"He never did those things. You'll see when you read it."

"He says so?"

"When you read it you'll see what I mean. He loved Clarice. And God help him, he loved you, too." She twisted her wedding ring. "There are other things in there."

"What things."

"I'll let you find out for yourself." She looked towards the window where sunlight was coming in through the curtains, breaking into irregular rays of gold and silver. The light behind her made her profile as defined as a cameo. "Just remember, he's dead. Clarice is dead. They're dead and buried." She went to the counter and tore a sheet of paper towel off a roll on a stand, folded it, and patted her eyes.

He could not remember when he'd last seen his mother cry. She had not cried when Clarice died, had not when his father died...at least, not where anyone could see her.

He pushed his chair back and stood. "I'll take it with me. Is that okay with you?"

She accompanied him to the door. He kissed her again on the cheek, and she touched his shoulder. "One thing, Alex. When you read it, try and keep an open mind."

"I'll try."

"It's important you do," she said.

Chapter 2

He did not want to go home. Miriam would be at her desk, writing lists of things to do, or working on the books of her shop. She was organized, one of the reasons for her success, but she had also had a good idea and had made it work. For several years before their son Richard was born, Miriam had worked in retail for a guy named Larry Mitler. Alex thought he was a smarmy, lecherous piece of shit but Miriam said she had no problem with him. Later, when Richard was older and in school, she had gone back to work part-time. Because Alex hated her working for Mitler and told her so *ad nauseum*, she had finally given it up. But she'd learned what it took to run a retail business.

When Richard was eighteen, he told them he was leaving home. "I want to try to live on my own," he'd said. They tried to talk him out of it using the usual arguments regarding safety, cost, comfort, and so on, all of which he shot down with resolute determination. Miriam didn't take it well. When Richard lived at home she was more or less anchored to the house. When he was gone she was at loose ends. Lunch and shopping with the girls was not something she wanted to do. After some time had passed, she decided to go into business for herself. She opened a shop dedicated to the traveler, called it "Voyager," and stocked it with specialized luggage, travel books, electrical converters, locks, travel alarms, gadgets of all kinds, and easy-care clothing. Before the opening, she plugged it with local advertising and direct mail, and from the first day she was doing steady business. She was proud of her accomplishment, and in spite of everything that was going on between them, so was he.

He drove back to their house in Lynbrook, pulling into the driveway at the side of the house. At one time, when Richard was beginning school, there had been other kids his age on the block, and in good weather they would be outside playing. In those days the mothers were around during the week, and fathers on weekends. But the block had grown old. The kids had grown up and moved away, and now all there was to see were the perfectly groomed lawns, signatures of the neatly kept homes, but everything as desolate as a graveyard.

He got out of the car and took his father's notebook from the passenger seat. He put it under his arm and went in the side door that led to a mudroom, then to the kitchen. He smelled something sweet and as he passed through the kitchen felt heat radiating from the oven. In the den he found Miriam sitting at the desk she had found in a junk shop and then restored. "What smells so good?" he asked.

"Brownies. I decided to whip up a batch."

He didn't care much for sweets, but Miriam's brownies were something special. He held the notebook out in front of him. "Know what this is?"

"Hardly. But you want me to ask, so I will. What is it?"

"A diary. Written by Max Gunther."

She whistled. She was a good whistler, could even put two fingers in her mouth and whistle loud enough to make your ears hurt.

"My mother found it. That's why she wanted me to come over."

"What's in it?"

"I don't know. I haven't read it yet."

"How come?"

"I'm not sure. I'm not even sure I want to read it."

"I can see it's bothering you. You look funny. Your lips are gray like you're going to walk the last mile."

He laughed. "That's how I feel."

"Maybe you ought to think about it then. Maybe reading the words of a dead man might not be such a good idea. It might bring a curse upon you."

"A curse from beyond the grave, you mean?"

"Exactly."

"Remember who wrote these words, okay. The man of curses, himself. Whatever he had to say from beyond the grave couldn't be worse than what he had to say when he was alive."

"Just giving you fair warning," she said. "Do what you want. You always do."

಄ಌ಄

The beginning had been so good. A beautiful fall day in the Village. Washington Square Park. 1952. He had been away for two years. His sister Clarice's death had carved an important part out of him. He had left school, bought a bus ticket to Dayton, Ohio because it sounded like a good place to be lost. From there he went on to other small towns—Muncie, Indiana, Springfield, Illinois, Ames, Iowa, Lincoln, Nebraska. He kept going until he finally ran out of country and decided to come back. He had given up living in shabby rooms, working odd jobs, trying to be anonymous. He came back to the familiar world, inhabited by people like his father, but no longer inhabited by Clarice.

He had graduated in Albany and gotten a job teaching science at Claremont, a private school in New Jersey.

Some weekends he went to the city.

"It wasn't Washington Square," he could hear Miri arguing. "It was in the Strand, the bookstore."

They'd had this argument many times. He claimed he had picked *her* up in the Square. She insisted she had picked *him* up in the bookstore.

Wherever it was, he knew immediately she was important. It wasn't that he had instantly fallen in love. It was more like he had been bee-stung or had touched a live wire.

She had asked him if he wanted to go for coffee. They went to One Fifth Avenue, where they were kept waiting behind a rope although they could see empty tables near a window.

"What's the matter with those?" Miriam asked the would-be actor who was keeping them waiting. He held a stack of menus in his hand.

"They're reserved."

"For Cary Grant, no doubt," Miriam whispered to Alex.

She flashed the menu-holder a dazzling smile. You could tell that she knew she had a great smile. "Please," she implored. "We're starving. We've been making love all night and we're ravenous. Please give us a table. I promise we'll eat fast."

The man behind the rope laughed. "That's a good one. Original. What the hell. Go ahead. Take any one you want."

When they were seated, she said, "I hate that."

"Hate what?"

"Having to charm someone to get what I want."

"Do you do that a lot?" Alex asked.

"Only when I need to."

"And does it always work?"

She smiled. Not a dazzler this time, a small one. "Oh, yes. I always get what I'm after. You better watch out if I decide to go after you."

When he went home that night he knew a lot about her. She was an only child. Lived with her widowed mother in a four-room apartment in Brooklyn Heights. Had a job selling in Macy's while she was deciding whether or not to go to college. She was nineteen.

✍✍✍

Alex took the diary down to the basement along with his pipe, tobacco, matches, and an ashtray. There was no other place in the house where he felt completely private. A long time ago he had paneled one part of it and made that into a game room for Richard and his friends. It had not been used in years. There was a Ping-Pong table, now warped, the edges scarred from paddle hits. A dartboard hung on the wall, one dart still stuck in it, and there was an old couch and armchair they'd moved downstairs after they'd bought new ones.

He sat in the armchair, the notebook unopened on his lap. He was anxious to read it, wasn't he? So why didn't he pick it up and start? He had read a few diaries, those written by famous people or people who became famous because of their diaries. *The Diary of Anne Frank,* of course. He remembered how affected he had been by her words, the beautiful innocence of her feelings. He'd also read some of Samuel Pepys, that horny old Englishman from the 17th century who managed to record almost everything he saw, felt, or heard, including his bowel movements. And some dirty ones when he was a hot teenager looking for any sex he could get. *My Secret Life by an Anonymous Victorian* was full of stiff pricks and bums and cunts and fucked her once and once again and yet again. He had been too young then to question the narrator's ability to get hard so many times. And there was Fanny Hill detailing erotic adventures from a woman's point of view even though it was written by a man. There were other diaries and many books he'd wanted to read, as well, and had not gotten to either. Same for movies and plays. The only time he'd really gotten excited was when he'd seen *Death of a Salesman* on Broadway. That was something like twenty years ago. Maybe he had a problem he'd never identified: interest, but not enough commitment to follow through.

His hands were cold. He filled his pipe, put a match to it, and got it going. He pulled in the smoke. It was funny— or not so funny—that Miriam had only just recently told him she couldn't stand his pipe.

ᏂᏆᏂ\

It was the day of his father's funeral. It had not been a good day; there had been too much not being said. Miriam was getting dressed and he had held the pipe in his hand.

"Please don't light that in here. I can't stand it," she said.

"Since when?"

"It makes the whole bedroom smell. The smoke gets into my clothes. If you want to smoke that thing, do it in the bathroom or downstairs at least."

"You used to say you loved the smell of pipe tobacco."

"I used to say a lot of things."

She pushed a small brush into a palette of color and then applied it in smooth strokes to her face. The ritual had always intrigued him. Clarice had even let him observe. There was the mystery in the combination of lotions, powders, pigments, and the perfumed smell of them. It was part of women's otherness: their exotic scents, their soft underwear, their circuitous minds.

She wore a simple black dress to match the occasion, a single strand of pearls around her neck, and matching pearl earrings. And, of course, the silver bracelet he'd bought her in Taxco. They'd taken a vacation in Mexico to celebrate their fifth anniversary and were still very much in love. She'd worn it almost daily since. When something stressed her she had a habit of twisting it.

"Beautiful," he remembered saying. "You look beautiful," seeing her shoulders lift slightly, proudly.

☙❧

He felt his jaw tighten as he finally opened the notebook. Instead of reading, he began turning pages to get an idea of how much there was to read.

The first thing he noticed was that his father had not written any dates. Each entry started on a different page but no time was indicated. Some of the entries were just a line, some a paragraph. He went through the notebook and saw that no entry was more than two pages long. Taken altogether not much more than a quarter of the pages had any writing on them. His father's handwriting slanted backward, the letters spindly and wavering as if they were written with an arthritic hand. But he knew his father never had arthritis in his hands; his pain was elsewhere. What the backward slant indicated, according to handwriting experts Alex had read, was a repressed personality. In his father's case, there was no doubt of its accuracy.

He began to read. Almost immediately he felt himself drawn as if he were being sucked into a whirlpool. The words reached out and filled him with a dizzying assortment of feelings and emotions that kept him reading so intensely he could hardly breathe. He read without stopping until he finished. Only then did he realize his pipe was cold.

Alex looked up and saw the poster Richard had tacked on the wall when they were fixing up the room. Alfred E. Newman smiled his "What, me worry?" smile. There was a musty dampness in the air.

He turned as if somebody was in the room with him as if he felt the need to talk to someone. "What is this?" he wanted to ask. This can't be my father. That stiff, unyielding man? With another woman? And then he thought, my mother read this. She read it and she wanted me to read it.

Why?

He read it through again, this time more slowly, examining every word as if each one had an underlying meaning.

When he was done he closed his eyes and took a deep breath. A moment later he snapped the notebook shut and knocked the ashes out of his pipe. He started up the stairs but stopped halfway, returned, and even though there was no one in the house but Miriam, he felt the need to hide the notebook under the cushion of the chair.

Chapter 3

His feet were cold but his face was hot as if he'd gotten a bad sunburn. He went into the bathroom and splashed cold water on his face. When he came out, Miriam said, "Finished already?"

He nodded.

"Well?"

"Don't ask me anything yet. I'm in a state of shock."

"That's not fair," she said. "Tell me *something*."

"I'll tell you this much. I've got another sister."

"What?"

"That's right. My father, of all people, had a child with another woman."

"That *is* a surprise. But why should it shock you? I thought every man does that kind of thing. Not have a baby, of course, but the affair."

She seemed to be looking at him with more than a hint of irony as if she knew his secret, knew that he had contemplated breaking faith with her. He hadn't yet, although he couldn't deny the temptation was there. Was it because he was a wuss, too scared to charge ahead? Or was his commitment too strong to break? Either way, he hadn't broken the marriage vow yet and at this moment he was glad of it. He said, "Not *my* father. Weren't you the one who called him the coldest son-of-a-bitch you ever met? Hardly the type to have a love affair."

"Maybe he wasn't as cold as I thought. Anyhow, what I meant about his coldness was why the two of you never got along. It didn't have anything to do with sex."

"You knew why we didn't get along. Or maybe you forgot."

"Of course I didn't forget. Nobody could forget anything like that. I just couldn't believe it."

"Jesus Christ. All these years, and you never told me that?"

"Let's say I was skeptical. From what I saw of your father and your mother, it just didn't seem to fit. I didn't tell you because I didn't want to hurt your feelings."

"That's a good one. I spill my guts to you about my father and my sister but you never bothered to tell me you thought I was full of shit."

"You were overwrought about it. You weren't about to listen to another point of view. I didn't want to be the opposition."

"Why not? That's what you are now, aren't you? And you know what? It makes sense. It's a perfect symbol of our relationship. Or what's become of it."

He walked away from her and went into the kitchen where he sat at the butcher-block table. The kitchen was oven-warm and the aroma of baking was pleasant but not strong enough to erase the bad memories they were talking about or to arouse good ones.

Miriam followed and sat across from him. He placed his hands on the table and looked at them. They looked strange to him, almost as if they belonged to somebody else.

"Is there anything in there about it? About Clarice?" she asked.

He nodded. "He writes about how much he loves her. He even talks about that night. The one I told you about a hundred times. Swears he never did anything. He even lies to himself!"

"What does he say?"

He shook his head. "Says he had feelings but didn't do anything. Right. Like I would believe it."

"It's possible."

"Why are you always defending him?"

"I'm not. I'm just doing what I've always done, trying to get you to see another possibility."

⚬⚬⚬

They were married in the month of June. The first year they agreed on most things, from what to do in the bedroom to what to cook in the kitchen. The best sex he had ever had was the first six months with Miri. They did it at every opportunity and in every place they could think of. In the apartment, it was on the kitchen table and under the table. Standing up and lying down. Against a wall, in the shower, on the couch, on the floor. They had pulled over to the side of the road in the car more than once, doing different things in the front seat and the back seat. But it wasn't the quantity and it wasn't the variety that made it so special. It was that each time was better than the last so the incentive was to do more and more in the expectation that the incredible satisfaction would go on forever.

Of course, it didn't. After Richard was born, everything was different. The new baby brought a kind of havoc. They were no longer lovers, they were parents—pressure, fright, lack of money. Miri had gone back to work. He was jealous of Mitler, her boss. She told him nothing was going on but he could not keep his suspicions quiet.

Even the outside world intruded. The Soviets shot down a South Korean airliner, killing hundreds. Hundreds more American marines are killed by explosions in Lebanon. President Reagan establishes that Russia is the Evil

Empire and sends thousands of troops to invade the threatening country of Grenada. All this had to produce stress in everyday life so how could there not be fights that began over trifles? Personal attacks, stupid ones, about his clothing, his eating habits, about her not being home when he calls, her not having dinner ready.

$e/\infty c/\infty$

And now. Now their marriage had advanced to raw edges, bone scraping against bone.

"Look," Miriam said, softly, "I told you I didn't believe your father was capable of such a thing. That has nothing to do with whether you believed it or not."

"I don't see any difference."

"There's a big difference. You were young. Maybe you didn't know what you were seeing. Maybe you imagined some of it."

"I didn't imagine anything."

"Your sister never complained, did she?"

"I did a lot of reading about it. The abused child never says anything. They're too scared. They bury it. When they grow up, they've often forgotten everything that happened. But Clarice never forgot."

"I really wish I'd known her," she said.

"I wish you'd known her, too." He leaned forward, elbows on the table, and put his head into his hands. "I don't remember exactly how old I was, around ten, I think—but I knew something bad was going on."

"Be fair. You thought you knew."

"He came out of her room, walked up to where I was, and stared into my face. Didn't say a word."

"And you wanted to talk to Clarice, but the door was closed."

"I put my ear against the door and listened but I didn't

hear a sound. I went back to bed but I don't think I slept the whole night. I kept seeing the look on my father's face."

"If something was going on, your mother must have known. Wouldn't she have done something about it?"

"I don't know. My mother never talked to me. And I could never bring myself to talk to her about it until it was too late."

"Something like us, lately," she said.

"We used to talk a lot."

"So what happened?"

He shook his head, avoiding her eyes, and said nothing.

Not once during his marriage had he ever had an affair. A few mild temptations maybe, but nothing remotely serious. Until now. He had known guys who had fooled around and bragged about it, but he had never wanted to. It may have been because, in spite of his not wanting to be, he was too middle class, wound tight as steel cable. But it was also true that his marriage was important to him and being faithful was part of the deal.

Miriam had been distant for some time. He wasn't sure how long her remoteness had been developing but it had become more apparent after Richard left. Maybe the boy's departure had accelerated something that had been underneath the surface all along and it took his leaving to make it known.

"Would you mind if I read it?" Miriam asked.

"No. But I'm not ready to give it up yet."

"No problem. I'll wait until you are ready."

They ate dinner together, mostly in silence. She had made baked pork chops in a sweet and sour sauce, with mashed potatoes and green beans. He wasn't hungry and left most of it on the plate. He thought that after dinner he would go back and read the diary one more time, but he did not, even though he could feel the presence of it lurking down there like an octopus deep underwater, its long tentacles reaching out to pull him underneath the surface.

Chapter 4

Miriam was always up well before Alex's alarm went off. She had usually showered, dressed, had her black coffee, and unbuttered slice of whole-wheat toast, and was gone before Alex came downstairs. This morning when she awoke she was alone in bed. She hadn't heard Alex get up. When she went downstairs for breakfast she saw that he had already left the house. She knew he was upset about his father's diary. He'd probably had a restless night. God knows, she'd had enough of her own recently. In the past they would have shared that kind of thing, but not now. One more sign of their disconnect.

Her shop was in Hewlett, only fifteen minutes away so it was easy for her to be sitting at her desk hours before they opened. She'd carved a small office not much bigger than a closet out of the back of the store. With the door closed and the phones quiet she could concentrate on the enormous amount of detail it took to run a small retail business. It was work that for the most part could not be delegated because hiring staff to take care of all the tasks would not be cost-effective. It fell to Miriam to do all the buying, follow up on orders not filled, as well as dealing with the details it took to manage the returns of defective merchandise. She also oversaw the window displays, checked the invoices, wrote the checks, made sure the merchandise in the store was set up in the most attractive way, and found time to listen in on the salespeople to ensure they did their selling in a low key but not disinterested manner.

This morning she sat at her desk twisting the bracelet on her wrist. Annoyed with herself at that habit, she stopped, picked up a pen, and began doodling on a yellow legal pad. She made no attempt to concentrate on business. What was happening at home had taken control of her life. Besides her marriage, there was their son Richard to worry about. He had left home two years before with only a high school diploma.

"I feel like I've got to get out of here, Mom. Out of the suburbs and into the real world."

"How are you going to live? What are you going to do?" she'd said.

He gave her that funny smile that never failed to ignite a burst of love in her. She knew at once she couldn't keep him, this child who had grown into manhood. He was taller than Alex, with wide shoulders. He had deep-set hazel eyes under heavy brows and a kind of movie star look that made women stare at him as he passed.

"I'm going to be an actor," he said.

Oh God, she thought but knew enough not to say it out loud. "You never said anything about this before."

"No, but it's something I've been thinking about for a long time."

Yes, he was gorgeous, but he'd need a lot more than that to make it as an actor. She rarely saw him but he called every few weeks or so.

"Things are going okay, Mom," he usually said. He was always cheerful, and optimistic. He'd been taking acting lessons, working in restaurants to pay his way. He'd found friends to share an apartment with. "A guy and a gal. These are great people, Mom. I am so lucky. His name is Ja-Marcus Young and hers is Li Ling. They want to be actors, too." He lived in Greenwich Village and seemed to be more than satisfied with his life.

As his mother, she'd had to accept what he'd done, difficult as it was to give up her hopes and dreams for him. She'd pictured him going to an Ivy League college, getting a degree that would send him off on a career that satisfied all the goals of the middle class. She had never cared what path he might have chosen, doctor, lawyer, social worker, teacher. But not acting! What kind of life was that? What were the chances of making it, one in a hundred thousand? Especially now, in 1975 when the whole world seemed to be in flux, inflation rampant, the economy in shambles, and any kind of job hard to find.

She had never denied being of the middle class, never thought it insulting as Alex did. To Alex it meant malls, sit-coms, beer gut, and driving the fanciest car you could afford. He aspired to higher things, a liberal point of view, a social conscience, a bias against the nouveau riche, and the conspicuous consumption that went with it. What he didn't tell her but she knew instinctively from almost the first moment they met was that he was damaged goods, maimed in some sort of way. She felt a melancholy underneath the surface, even though he laughed a lot and had a good sense of humor. After a few dates, she asked him about it. He denied it was there.

"I guess I'm not the funniest guy in the world," he'd said. "And maybe I'm a little too serious about the world and what happens in it, but as for me personally, what have I got to be sad about? I found you, didn't I?"

She didn't believe him. At the same time, she suspected that it drew her to him the way it would if he were a wounded bird. It also helped that he had the most beautiful blue eyes and the longest lashes, that he wore tweed jackets with leather patches on the elbows and smoked a pipe with tobacco that smelled like peaches. He looked every bit the professor—in those days he was still teaching—and he cared about the poor, the homeless, and the disadvantaged, just as she did.

And now their marriage was coming apart. She was watching its failure and wasn't sure when it had started to fracture, wasn't sure why wasn't sure if she should fight to save it or let it go. She was like a pedestrian crossing the street who suddenly sees a truck barreling down on her and can't move to get out of the way. They'd had a lot of years together, twenty-two, in fact. There was a variation of the quality of those years that ranged from superior, to excellent, very good, good, and not so good. There had even been plenty of bad times, but they had stayed together, compromised, swallowed hard, and made it work.

But maybe enough was enough. Maybe it was time to give up, let go of the old and begin with the new. She was still young, only forty-one. A whole new life could be ahead of her, possibly even a new family. Why not? She wouldn't be the first to begin again at this age. Men did it all the time. Why not a woman?

On a sudden whim, she picked up the phone and dialed. She counted the rings out loud…four, five, six, seven, eight…okay, Ma, time to answer."

Her mother never picked up the phone before at least eight rings. Her explanation was, "If they don't want to wait to talk to me, I don't need to talk to them."

Her mother's raspy voice said, "Hello? Who is this?"

"It's your darling daughter."

"Hello, darling daughter. What's up?"

"Can you meet me for lunch? I need to talk."

"If you're buying, it's a deal."

Chapter 5

The clock read 5:10. He shut off the alarm knowing Miriam didn't need it and that he wouldn't be able to go back to sleep. He left the warmth of the bed they still shared and dressed in the dark. Miriam was not yet awake when he went back to the basement and retrieved the diary from under the chair cushion. Although he felt somewhat foolish doing it, he recognized the need to take it with him. On the walk to the Lynbrook train station, he found himself shivering. It was usually mild in October, but the air had a chill at that hour he wasn't used to.

He got a coffee at a deli and waited on the platform, along with the other commuters, holding the hot container in one hand and the notebook in the other. He wondered why he had brought it with him since there was no chance once work began that he would have the time or the opportunity to look at it. Had he been afraid to leave it behind or unable not to have it near him? Even through the cover, he imagined he could see the confined, slanted script of his father. Miriam had joked, half-seriously, about being cursed by reading the words of a dead man. Maybe she was right. He had to ask himself why his father had written the diary in the first place. Why had he left it where it was sure to be found? His mother told him she'd discovered it by accident. He couldn't help wondering about her truthfulness. She was always aware of what was going on around her. She was the original of the grown-up who said, "I have eyes in the back of my head." So how would she not have known about the diary? More important, how could she not have known about Clarice? He'd asked himself this question countless times.

His mother must have seen *something*. And if she had, wouldn't she have confronted his father? She wasn't afraid of him. Why would she be? To all appearances, his father ran the house. He was the master of all he surveyed—so he thought. But Alex knew differently. Somehow, his mother managed to have things go her way, at least when it was important to her.

He suddenly felt an urge for action. To hell with work. He left the railroad platform and walked all the way back to the house.

He could just get in his car and go but he knew Miriam was still home and felt he had to show himself. She looked up in surprise. "What's going on?"

"I have to do something. It's important."

"What do you mean?"

For some reason he didn't want to tell her. Maybe he feared that if he told her she'd ask questions and once he started explaining he'd lose the urgency he now felt. "I'll explain later."

He drove to Valley Stream. The front door was locked. It was always locked. He rang the bell. When his mother opened the door, her eyebrows lifted in surprise.

"Alex? Why are you here? Aren't you supposed to be at work?"

"I have to talk to you. It's very important."

"Come into the kitchen. I'm making something."

There was a buttery aroma in the air. Something was in the oven, probably a casserole. His mother was a great believer in casseroles.

"I see you have the diary with you," his mother said.

"I've been reading it. I've read it a few times already."

"So what do you think?"

The heat from the stove was making him more uncomfortable than he already was. "I don't know what to think. What I want is the truth. I don't believe you never saw anything go on between Dad and Clarice. I just don't believe it."

His mother sighed loudly. "Not again."

"Yes, again. How could you not have seen anything? How could you not have been at least suspicious?"

"Why should I have been suspicious?"

"All those nights his going into her room? What did you think he was doing in there?"

"He was concerned about her. He was afraid she was going to get into trouble. It was obvious she was a mixed-up little girl."

"Mom! For god's sake. She wasn't a little girl. She was becoming a teenager. Lots of kids that age are mixed up. And they don't need their fathers coming into their rooms at night to lecture them."

"Maybe not. But your father loved Clarice more than you can imagine. I know you weren't his favorite. And you probably resent that. But he felt she needed talking to."

"What did he think she was going to do? Become a professional shoplifter?"

"He was afraid she was going to ruin her life."

"How?" Alex said. "She'd never done anything terrible. Smoked cigarettes, that's all."

"He found alcohol in her room."

"Like booze, you mean?"

"A bottle of rye whiskey. It was under her mattress."

Alex felt the air go out of his lungs. "I don't believe it."

"It was half empty."

"So she drank a little. Is that so terrible?"

"Yes. Very much so. And you know it."

"It's so hard to believe," Alex said. "She would have told me. She told me everything."

"But she never told you anything bad about her father, did she?"

He shook his head.

"She never told you he molested her, did she?" His mother stood up and laid the palm of her hand against his cheek. "Go home, son. Get this out of your mind. What's done is done. Let her rest in peace."

Chapter 6

Miriam had arranged to meet her mother at a somewhat upscale restaurant in Hewlett, not far from her shop. She had chosen it because it wasn't as noisy as other nearby lunch places and they'd be able to talk. She walked slowly, trying to decide what she was going to say. She'd been occupied all morning and had not had time to do much thinking about it. In a strange way she was glad not to have had the time to think because now she was already sorry that she'd actually gone and called her mother. Not that she didn't want to talk to her mother, not that she didn't trust her. But her mother was so quick to make up her mind and so damn opinionated. Sometimes even before Miriam finished telling her something, she'd jump in with a response. She didn't have to think hard for an example. It happened almost every time she and her mother had a conversation.

The restaurant had a small bar on one side and dining room seating on the other. She told the young woman who came over carrying a handful of menus that she wanted a table for two but that the other person wasn't there yet.

"No problem," the young woman said. "You can wait at the bar or at a table."

Miriam chose a table near a window and sat down. She wasn't surprised that her mother was late. She was driving from Brooklyn and traffic was often a problem. When

Miriam once broached the idea of her moving, perhaps to be closer, her response was quick. "Why would I move? I love it here. I have a bunch of friends in the area and I know every shopkeeper by name. And, of course, they all know me."

Without a doubt, Miriam thought.

She was studying the menu when the familiar voice called from across the room. "I made it." She looked up to see her mother at the entrance, waving her hand. She wore a lavender blouse, an orange skirt, white shoes, and white clunky jewelry. As usual, she had on enough makeup to make Estee Lauder smile.

Her mother went around behind Miriam and kissed the top of her head before sitting down. "What a ride," she said, in a voice loud enough for the entire restaurant to hear. "That fucking Belt Parkway. The worst road ever, except of course, for the BQE and the Cross Bronx. Nothing can top those."

"Mom, the world is not interested in your opinion of the Belt Parkway."

"You mean, I'm a loud, foul-mouthed old lady? Tough shit. And how are you, darling daughter?"

"Fine. You look quite summery today, Mom. Did you forget it's October?"

"Listen, Miss Smarty-Pants, it's in the mid-seventies. To me, that's summer. Besides, you know I don't follow the rules of fashion."

"I think I know that by now. But you look nice anyway," Miriam said.

"I know I do. But you don't."

"Well, thank you very much."

"You know what I mean. I'm not talking about how you're dressed. You always look terrific. I'm talking about the look in your eyes."

"Cut it out, Mom. Just because I said I wanted to talk

to you, doesn't mean something terrible is happening."

"Glad to hear it. Then let's eat. I'm starving."

They ordered lunch. Miriam didn't drink when she was working but her mother had a vodka Gibson straight up. "No ice," she told the waitress. "Waters it down and kills the flavor."

"Just remember you're driving," Miriam said.

"Who's the mother and who's the daughter?" her mother replied.

Miriam laughed. "You never let up."

Her mother's hair was bleached a pale blonde and cut so that it framed her heart-shaped face like a halo, not unattractively. She was sixty-three and could pass for fifty. She wasn't as slim as she used to be but the curves were all in the right places. Her mother had been a widow since Miriam was a little girl, yet had never remarried. Miriam had asked her about it more than once. "Not interested," had been the reply.

The Gibson arrived along with Miriam's iced tea.

"Come on," her mother said, after a sip. "Let's hear it."

"I'd rather eat."

"Why are you stalling? You called *me*, remember?"

Miriam nodded and decided to lie. She had suddenly realized she wasn't ready to talk about Alex with her mother who hadn't been thrilled with her marrying him in the first place. Who knew what she'd expected for her only child? Perhaps some guy from an upper-class background. She'd never said, but it was surely not a guy teaching in a small private school, and in New Jersey, no less. So Miriam was not terribly surprised when, with great excitement, she announced her engagement, and the response was an unenthusiastic, "Wonderful, darling if he's what you want."

"Okay. It's about Richard." Lame, she thought, Mom already knows this. I have to do better. "He wants to be an actor. And…" she paused to drink from her glass while she thought of what to say next.

"I know all that. We've been through it before. What are you doing, getting upset about it again? I told you after he does a zillion auditions and gets turned down every time, he'll change his mind and get an honest job or go back to school."

"You think so?" Miriam didn't believe it would be this easy.

Her mother stared at her. "Wait a minute. Are you bull-shitting me?"

"Why would you say that?"

"You're not upset about Richard. Not enough to call and say you have to talk to me. It's something else, isn't it?" When Miriam didn't answer, she slapped the table. "I knew it."

Their orders arrived. "Did you say you were hungry?" Miriam said. She picked up her fork and began to eat.

They ate in silence for a while. Then her mother said, "Okay if you don't want to talk, I'll talk. I've got a boy-friend."

Miriam almost choked while trying to swallow. "What?"

"Boyfriend. You know what that is, the male of the spe-cies, two arms, two legs, and a—."

"Don't," Miriam said.

Her mother smiled.

"So tell me about it," Miriam said. "Who is he? How did it happen? How come you never said a word before this?"

"I wanted to make sure it worked out before I said any-thing. You know it's been a long time."

"I know. So let's hear it."

"I've known him a couple of weeks. He only recently moved into my building. That's where I met him. In the elevator."

"He picked you up?"

"Nothing like that. He said hello, that's all. I said hello back."

"And? Then what?"

"Nothing. He told me he had moved into the building and wanted to introduce himself. Which he did. I got off at my floor and he said he hoped he would run into me again. I said that would be nice, so long for now, and that was that."

"God, this is like pulling teeth," Miriam said. "Get to the meaty part."

"You're too young to hear that."

"God forbid you should tell me. How did you get to-gether? Did he call you? Knock on your door? Ask you out? What? And what's his name and how old is he?"

"Relax, bubbeleh. You'll upset your stomach if you get too excited."

Miriam shook her head in frustration. "I will not say one more word."

"He's a widower. His name is Henry Mancini. Right. He's not Jewish and he's not the composer."

"He'd hardly be living in your building if he was."

"He says he's related, though. And he's very musical. Dances like a dream."

"He took you dancing?"

Her mother nodded. "How about that? I wanted to see a Broadway play but the musicians' strike is still on. So we went to Roseland. I've always been on the side of un-ions. Your grandfather was a union man, you know."

"I thought he owned the hardware store Daddy worked in."

"That was later. When he was young he was in the plumbers union."

"I always liked it when Grandpa came to visit. He used

to read me bedtime stories."

"What are you saying, *I* never read you stories?"

"I didn't say that, but now you mention it, you didn't. Daddy did."

"When did I have time to read to you? I was taking care of the house, paying the bills, doing everything."

"Mom, calm down. I'm not accusing you of anything. I'm more interested in Roseland."

"Oh yes, he took me to Roseland. It was lovely. We had a wonderful time."

"Great."

"And what a gentleman. Brought me a corsage. Holds the door for me. Stands up when I come back from the ladies' room."

"Sounds too good to be true. But I'm really glad for you. Can I get to meet this charming gentleman?"

"Of course. I'll make a dinner party. You and Alex, me and Henry. What do you think?"

For the moment she wasn't sure what to say. She and Alex. With all that was now going on between them? Together at a dinner party with her mother and her new boyfriend? That didn't sound promising. On the other hand, maybe that was just what she needed, something that would force her forward, away from her passivity. She would have to tell Alex about the party and hope to get his cooperation. She could use that as a beginning and then find a way to segue to talk about what was happening to them.

"Great idea, Mom," she said. "I can hardly wait."

Chapter 7

He called the office and told them he'd been delayed. When he got there everyone was busy—Ruth, Esther, Billie, and Wanda, who was Mr. Roth's private secretary. They all worked in one room. There were five desks, phones on each, wastebaskets full at the end of the day. There were glaring fluorescents overhead and the off-white walls had been in need of paint for a long time. His boss, Stuart Roth, who liked being called Mister Roth, even though he was several years younger than Alex, had the only private office.

Wanda's desk was just outside Roth's door and she had a telephone with an intercom so Roth could tell her things without anyone hearing. Often she was inside with the door closed for what seemed an unusually long time and Alex used to be sure something hot was going on, even though Roth seemed to have no interest in women or in anything else other than money. Alex used to picture her lying on the desk, her hair falling back, her knees in the air with Roth between them. But now he was pretty sure it had all been his fired-up imagination. Maybe because he wanted it to be him between her knees on the desk.

He slipped the notebook into his desk drawer. He tried to get into the details that constituted his job. Ruthie had already opened the mail. He sorted it according to task—invoices to Ruthie, checks to Esther, orders, complaints, solicitations, and junk to Billie. Then he usually went into the factory to check production with Luis, the foreman.

There were twelve workers in addition to Luis. Their most popular item was a Paul Revere bowl. They made it in six sizes, and sold it to Macy's, Fortunoff, and the Spiegel catalog, as well as hundreds of gift shops across the country. That object accounted for 60% of their business, so keeping track of its production was fundamental. The shop was non-union but when he picked up a rumor that a union was out to organize them and passed on the rumor to his boss, the man had a fit. "They'll kill us! They'll organize us right out of business! Can you do anything about it?"

"I don't know. Right now all I can do is keep an eye on it."

He found Luis in the back of the shop, the customary toothpick in his mouth. "We doing good," the foreman said, even before Alex asked.

They were surrounded by machines and the smell of chemicals and the emery dust used for polishing. "Bullshit. You guys are fucking off back here. Cut out the tequila and beer at lunch." Alex winked and knuckled Luis in the stomach. He had a belly that hung over his belt, but it was surprisingly hard. "What do I hear about the union coming around?"

Luis acknowledged, "They been here."

"So what do you think? Are the guys interested?"

"We runnin' low on silver," Luis said, avoiding his question.

"Okay," Alex said. He would have to go slowly. He didn't know where Luis stood.

"*Comprende.* I'll talk to you later."

The door to Roth's office was open.

"When's he coming in, Wanda? Did he call?" He was all business in front of the others, fearing somehow that what he sometimes fantasized might show.

"I never know," she said. "He comes in whenever he comes in."

There were papers all over her desk. He didn't know what they were. Roth gave her busy work because he didn't really need a secretary. It was another ego trip for him, just as he had to have the 700 Series BMW and wear only Bally on his feet.

He thought again of his mother and Clarice. In spite of his mother's denials, he wondered if Clarice had ever told her anything. He guessed she might have because the two of them had a relationship that was far different from the one he had with his mother. There was closeness between them that had never been granted to him.

He could remember once, in the good times, finding the two of them at the kitchen table, posed like a Vermeer, their heads inclined towards each other, an aura of sweetness around them. Clarice, with her own pair of knitting needles and the basket on the table with balls of yarn, yellow, brown, orange, and his mother saying gently to her, as the needles clicked together, "That's wonderful, Clary, you're doing such a good job."

He glanced at Wanda. Shining hair. The familiar perfume. Only a hint of makeup. She had a clean, scrubbed, preppie look. He had guessed when he first saw her that she was probably around thirty-five. Her hair was more reddish than brown, and he assumed she colored it. She wore it in a casual way, much the same as Miri, hanging loose down to her shoulders, sometimes with a ribbon in it, sometimes pulled into a ponytail. Today she was wearing navy trousers, a plain white shirt, and a man's navy tie stippled with white. It was intended to be a masculine look but what it really said was, "I'm sexy and I know it."

He'd wanted to see her before, but now he felt an urgency to be with her. Lunch would be the best time. He could hardly ask her in front of the other women. They were in thrall to gossip. They chattered all day about the foibles of others. He knew, as well, that he was under constant observation, one of the two roosters in the henhouse. He decided to drop a note on her desk as if it were a work order from Mr. Roth. Ask her to leave early for lunch. They could meet at *John's*. It was a diner the girls in the office despised, greasy, ugh! which made it an ideal choice.

He wrote the note and after a while handed it to her. "Mr. Roth left this for you."

"Oh? Why didn't he give it to me himself?"

"Don't ask me," he said, going back to his desk.

She read it quickly. "Okay. It's nothing. I'll take care of it."

He had no idea what she meant or what she would do.

The morning went by slowly. It was not difficult to do the work because he did it mechanically, with little concentration. He felt a headache coming on, swallowed a couple of aspirin, and began checking credit on the orders that had come in over the weekend. Some of the reps had a habit of writing orders for people who couldn't get credit for two pairs of shoelaces, much less their $1000 minimum.

His eyes strayed to the drawer of his desk where the notebook lay in wait for him and then to his wristwatch to see the slow crawl to the lunch hour.

When he looked up to glance at Wanda, she seemed to be distracted. One moment she was typing, the next moving papers around on her desk. She suddenly pushed her chair back and announced that she was going to lunch.

Ruthie said, "It's kinda early, isn't it? It's only 11:30."

"I can't help it. I'm starving." She slipped on her jacket and quickly left.

"What's with her?" one of the other women asked.

"Maybe she's got a date."

"Who with? Robert Redford?"

"Too young for her."

"Meow, meow."

"Ladies, ladies," Alex called out. "Give me a break. I'm trying to get something done here."

"Well, so are we," Ruthie laughed. "Mr. Spoil Sport."

At noon, Ruthie and Esther went to lunch leaving Billie to answer the phone and watch the office. Alex waited ten minutes, then he stood up and put on his suit jacket. He rarely left the office, and usually had a sandwich at his desk.

"You're going out to lunch?" Billie said. "That's a change."

"I've got some things I have to do."

He was sure Billie would tell the others he went out, which would give them something to yak about, but so be it, he couldn't worry about everything.

The factory was downtown in a busy industrial area, not far from Canal Street. He walked quickly, crossing streets in front of taxis, and trucks, inhaling the odors of exhaust pipes and roasting chestnuts. She was in a booth, a cup of coffee sitting on a paper placemat in front of her, seemingly lost in thought. He was happy to see her there, but when they made eye contact, her expression didn't change.

He slid onto the bench opposite her. "I'm glad you came."

"I came because you asked me to. No other reason."

"I need to talk to someone. I thought you'd listen."

"What do you want to talk about?"

Before he could answer, the waitress came over. "Have you decided?"

He picked up the menu, a typical diner catalog encased in plastic, lunch specials on 3x5 cards. Wanda said I'll have chicken salad on whole-wheat toast."

Alex ordered a BLT, mayo on the side.

When the waitress left, Wanda said, "I meant to ask, aren't you still supposed to be sitting *shiva*?"

"How do you know about that? *Shiva*?"

"I grew up with Jews. I had more Jewish friends than my own kind."

"We didn't sit *shiva*," he said. "We never did anything that had to do with religion. My father didn't believe in it. I wasn't even bar-mitzvah'd."

"Oh."

She said it wearily, and now he could see a mournfulness about her that he hadn't seen before. He felt a sudden desire to put his arms around her, draw her close, maybe put his mouth on her warm neck. He was pretty sure she wouldn't object, almost sure she'd been coming on to him. There had been signals: body language, heat in their eye contact. She'd been working in the office for almost a year but it was only recently he'd paid attention. He'd been attracted to other women in the past but had never done anything about it. Why now? Maybe it had something to do with his being forty-five. Maybe he was a walking cliché, a man going through a midlife crisis. Maybe he needed to something more in the way of sex. He and Miri hadn't had sex in months. In fact, he couldn't remember the last time they'd fucked.

"Something wrong?" he asked.

"It's my mother. She's not well."

"I'm sorry."

"She has cancer."

"Shit."

"Exactly. I just found out about it. She called me last night and told me."

"How old is she?"

"Young. Fifty-five."

"Only ten years older than I am. So why don't I feel

young?"

"We're not talking about you."

"I'm sorry. I didn't mean it that way."

"It's breast cancer," she said.

"They have a high rate of cure for that, don't they?"

"It all depends on how far it's spread."

"Do you have family who can help you with this?"

"My father and my daughter. They don't know yet."

"I assume you're going to tell them."

"My mother asked me to keep it to myself for a while."

The waitress set their plates down in front of them.

"I don't think I'm hungry," Wanda said.

"Neither am I. Why don't we go?"

He left a twenty on the table and they went outside. The sun was bright; it had gotten considerably warmer than it had been in the morning. It was one of those October days in New York that made the world special. The sky was gentian-blue, with a few cumulus clouds drifting across, and the air soft and warm. He put his face up to the sun and took a breath trying to get some pleasure out of it, but there was too much opposition for it to work.

He put his hand on her arm and they began to walk in no particular direction. After a while, he took her hand in his.

"Do you think that's a good idea?" Wanda asked, but she didn't withdraw her hand.

"We're just holding hands."

"Someone might see us and think something else."

"Let them. We haven't done anything wrong."

"Not yet."

"Are you thinking we might?" he asked.

"Are you?"

"I asked you first."

She didn't answer, and they continued walking. "I just remembered," she said. "You wanted to tell me something.

I never gave you a chance."

He was confused for a moment, not sure of why he had asked her to be here in the first place. Ostensibly, it was to tell her about the diary. Maybe that was the reason and maybe it wasn't. He suddenly felt an overwhelming desire to tell her all kinds of things: about his boyhood, his feelings about his sister and his father. He wanted her to listen to how he felt about his wife and his mother and the diary and what he'd already learned from it. All this was filling him up and ready to burst out of him, but as abruptly as it had come, the feeling vanished. He realized that what she had learned about her mother had devastated her. What would anything he had to say mean to her now? "Let's save it for another time," he said.

Chapter 8
1943

Beginning at about the sixth grade and continuing through high school there were calls home about Clarice. Your daughter is fresh, she yells, talks back. When you think she's in school she's not. She's cutting classes. Clarice was found smoking in the bathroom, again. There were also a few occasions when certain items that belonged to other people were found in her possession—a bracelet, a watch, a ring. She was never expelled, although he knew she came close. His father would take time off, go down to the school and talk to the principal. Whatever he said or did, it worked. The worst she ever got was a few days' suspension.

Only he, the brother, knew about her shoplifting in stores because she never got caught. She kept the loot in her room. Sometimes she would show him what she had scored. It was mostly small stuff, like candy and gum, or cheap jewelry. Once in a while, she would swipe something bigger: a tee-shirt, or a pair of jeans.

"Why?" he asked.

"It's fun."

"What if you get caught?"

"I won't."

Clarice believed the stars in the heavens controlled destiny. When he was twelve and she was sixteen, she told him: "The moment you were born, the moment you took your first breath, it's called the prana, it was all decided. The Universe is One Living Being with one material substance and one Spirit. Marcus Aurelius said that."

She had taken him outside at night to look at the sky. "There it is. Look at that sight. Isn't it fabulous?" Her voice was dreamy as if she were up there in that vastness among the galaxies along with the stars and the planets. "Everything we want, everything we dream of is decided by those heavenly bodies. Doesn't that sound wonderful? Heavenly bodies."

She told him how stars were formed, how the earth was made, and how the light he was seeing from a distant star had begun traveling toward them thousands of years before. She told him about Nostradamus and that the predictions he had made in the 16th century, all based on the constellations, had come true.

"Is that possible?" he had asked.

"Absolutely. You have to know how to cast a horoscope and, of course, how to read one. I'm not Nostradamus, but I can tell you a lot."

"You can predict my future?"

"Not this minute. It takes a lot of time. Right now, I can tell you this. You're a Taurus. That means you've got a lot of good qualities. It signifies you're a loyal person. You're very caring. Sometimes you have a tendency to be stubborn, and you get overly emotional about things. Some other stuff, too."

"What other stuff?"

"I have to cast your horoscope first. There's a lot involved. It's not just the day you were born, it's the time you were born...the moment of your prana. At that exact moment, all the cosmic energy around you was absorbed into you. And exactly where you were born is important, too. That means the longitude and latitude. Then I have to look up the positions of the planets. Also, the exact placement of the Earth in space in relation to the Zodiac."

"Boy! You really know all that stuff?"

She nodded, "Yes." She told him about the Zodiac and the signs, the triplicities, and the elements of earth…air… fire…water.

"Did you do yours?"

"Of course. I'm a Scorpio. House of Mars, but Venus was involved. That makes me what I am. I accept it."

"What do you accept?"

"My future."

"You know your future?"

"Yes. Something very interesting is going to happen."

"What is it?"

She shook her head.

"Come on. You can tell me."

She smiled but wouldn't say more.

He wondered if she really knew.

Chapter 9

When he got back from work that evening, Miriam was still not home. He had a fleeting thought that he was being ridiculous but he still felt compelled to take the diary and go straight to the basement. He had not considered opening it on the train surrounded by strangers with curious eyes. He switched on the lamp, filled his pipe, got it going, and began to read it again from the beginning.

I know I'm starting off wrong. I bought this book because of what happened. But I can't get myself to write it down.

The second page:

I want to write down what I feel. I need to do this. I cannot tell anybody what I have done. I do not want to hurt anyone.

I write in the basement because I know I will have privacy. Nobody asks me what I am doing down here because my workshop is here and I am always doing something. Besides, nobody is interested in what I am doing. They are glad if I am out of their way. My family. A wife and two children. And a house. All I could ask for. The American

Dream. So why do I feel that it is all for nothing?

F. told me she is pregnant. I am cursed. I know it. Is it because I have denied God all my life? Is there someone really who watches us? No. I don't believe it. I won't believe it. But why does this happen? Only a few moments of forbidden love. A few moments of weakness. One moment of moral failure in a lifetime. Is this fair?

She is going to have the baby. I am not surprised because I knew she was a good Catholic. She comes from an Italian family that would sooner see her die than get rid of the baby. I told her I will help. She says all right but we will never see each other again, at least not in that way. Of course. I did enough damage already. I don't want to make it worse for her. Maybe she can find somebody to marry her and give the baby a father. A better father than I would be!!!

Three large exclamation points were scrawled after the last line with such force that the paper was torn.

When Alex came once more to the three stabbed exclamation points he paused, took a deep breath, then turned the page.

I never thought it would come to this. I never thought. Period. How could I do such a thing?

After that were several pages with just brief sentences or phrases written on them. Some were questions, cries for answers.

What am I doing?

Is it wrong?

I feel nothing but love. I am glad we made a baby, another life. Maybe it will be a good one.

It is real. Not fake. This love of mine.

How can it be bad? We created a new life.

Then there were some blank pages before one appeared almost all taken up with the small, backward strokes of his father's handwriting.

I see her every day. I pass by the assembly area where she works. I look at her belly to see if there's any sign of it.

She sees me looking at her. I know she doesn't like it because nobody knows about us and she wants to keep it that way. Sure. So do I.

Sometimes I want to tell the world. I'm the one. It's me who made love to this beautiful young woman. Me!

And it was exciting. I think maybe because it wasn't married love.

I knew in my heart it wouldn't end good, but I didn't care.

Alex thought about Wanda and the excitement of clandestine love. Is that what he was looking for? He couldn't deny his cock hardening when he thought about her. When was the last time that had happened with Miri?

I didn't write here for a long time. It must be months. I got used to the idea of what happened. I made up my mind it was finished and that was that. She's not in the shop anymore. They say she went to visit relatives out of state. She went somewhere to have the baby, that's for sure. I hope everything will be all right.

Another page:

I know she was the one who started it. She gave me the eye. Why did she do that? I never went after any of the girls in the shop. Or anywhere else for that matter. So why me? Did she guess I was a starving man? I don't know.

Alex turned the page. Blank. The next page, also blank. Why did he skip pages? Now he came to what he'd read more than once.

I love my daughter. I love her so much. She is my life. I wish I felt the same about my son. But we do not see eye to eye. We are strangers, even enemies, in the same house.

He leaned back with the notebook on his lap. He realized he'd been sitting rigid as copper pipe. Exploring his father's writing trying to find hidden meanings in the words was like stumbling through a forest of brambles and vines. He needed a break. His eyes closed…

⌘⌘

He had heard giggling and sprinkles of laughter coming from the bathroom. He had walked in there to find Clarice in the tub with his father. His father had a mass of hair on his chest; his arms were covered with hair and there was an abundance of it across his back, thick and shining with drops of water.

Clarice was eight then, four years older than he. Dad was soaping her with a washcloth and tickling her. Alex was jealous, he wanted to get in the tub with them.

Clarice laughed and squealed, twisting and turning.

Neither of them paid any attention to him, until he cried, "I want to play, too. Can't I play, too?"

"Not now, Alex," his father said. "You go away now."

He ran downstairs to find his mother. She had a dust rag in her hand and was wiping the top of the dining room table. "Mommy, Clary, and Daddy are having a bath. Can't I have one, too?"

She stopped her dusting and gave him a strange look. He wasn't sure if it meant she was annoyed or angry. "Not now, Alex. Can't you see I'm busy? I'll give you a bath after dinner."

"But I want one now," he cried.

His mother resumed her dusting and didn't answer him.

ᥱ᛭ᥱ᛭ᥱ

The door at the top of the stairs opened and Miriam called down, "Are you okay? You've been down there a long time."

"What time is it?"

"Time to eat. Are you hungry? I know I am."

"Sure."

There was a memory pulling at him. Something was there but what it was eluded him. He turned off the floor lamp and went up the steps. A jacket that had been hanging on a hook had fallen. As he bent to pick it up he felt a pain in his low back. Age, as well as the past, was closing in on him. "Don't look back," Satchel Paige had said. "Something might be gaining on you."

He tossed the notebook onto the kitchen table and sat down heavily.

"Still reading it?" Miriam asked.

He sighed. "I can't seem to stop."

"Why don't you give it a rest? Forget about it for a while? Think dinner. Nourishment. How about some takeout fried chicken?"

"Fine."

He went to KFC to get the chicken but he was unable to take her advice. He couldn't stop thinking about Clarice and his father, the woman named F., and the sibling he now knew existed somewhere in the world.

He would have eaten out of containers but that was not Miriam's style. She put the chicken, coleslaw, and fries into serving dishes and set the table in the kitchen with plates, napkins, and cutlery. She opened a bottle of white wine. In spite of all that was on his mind, he ate with appetite.

After he'd swallowed the last of his wine, Alex pushed back his chair and said he was going to continue with the diary.

"Aren't you being a little obsessive about it?" Miriam said.

"I'm being a lot obsessive."

"You could talk to me instead," Miriam said. "We could talk to each other."

"There doesn't seem to be anything to talk about."

"Are you serious? There's a million things to talk about."

He sighed. He didn't want to get into this now, but he knew she was right.

"How about this, for starters?" Miri went on. "My mother has a boyfriend and she's invited us to have dinner with her to meet this guy. What do you say to that?"

Alex stared at her for a moment, absorbing what she'd said. He smiled. "Really?"

"Really."

"Wow! When did this come about?"

"Not too long ago, apparently."

"I think that's great."

"Does that mean you'll go when the time comes?"

"Of course. I wouldn't want to disappoint Mabel. You know I'm crazy about her."

Miriam swirled the wine in her glass. "She doesn't know anything about us. I mean, what's been happening."

"What do you mean, happening?"

She sipped the wine. "You know very well what I mean. Our marriage. Where it's going. Or where it went."

"This isn't a good time to talk about it."

"You're wrong. It's the perfect time to talk about it."

"I'm sorry," Alex said. "I can't." He stood up.

"That's right. Walk away. Go hide in the basement. Read your damn diary. Get lost in the past. Is that going to solve anything?"

"Jesus Christ! What do you want from me? I can't think about anything else. I know I'm obsessed but I need to understand what that son of a bitch meant by writing what he did. Until then, everything else will have to wait."

Chapter 10

Alex refilled his pipe and lit it, sucking hard, pulling smoke into his lungs. He felt like a piece of shit. He'd always prided himself on being honest with himself and with others. But he'd left Miri alone in the kitchen, knowing he'd told her a half-truth. He could deal with the diary. He couldn't deal with their marriage. He still wasn't sure what had gone wrong or even when it had begun to go wrong. Two years ago they'd celebrated their 20th wedding anniversary. They'd gone into the city to celebrate. Man of La Mancha and the Four Seasons, filet mignon, and to hell with the expense. As far as he knew there were no problems. They'd gone home and made love and all seemed to be well. So what happened since?

Miri had shaken him when she said she wanted to talk about their marriage, though he shouldn't have been surprised. They'd come close to recognizing there were problems but had somehow put off discussions. He couldn't remember the last time they'd had a talk that had to do with just them and not one that dealt with their son or family or her business. In the beginning, of course, that was all they talked about. How wonderful their lives were. How lucky they were that they had each other. There were no thoughts other than that they would be together forever.

He sat on the old chair in the basement. The cushion was worn so that the springs pushed uncomfortably into his ass. He was torn between thinking of his past and the past of the man who had written the diary he held in his hands. In spite of himself he opened the cover and began reading it again.

I have this feeling in my gut. I think she planned to have this baby all the time. I remember once she says why bother, wouldn't it be nice to do it natural. I knew it was dumb but I couldn't stop myself. It was heaven on earth. She said, any time, Maxie, any time, but I didn't. I didn't give in to temptation again, that one time was enough.

The next page:

I've been doing a lot of thinking. I'm pretty sure now it was all a trick. She didn't love me. She never said she loved me. I never told her I loved her. But I did. Now I think I hate her, too.

Another page:

I could never hate her. She gave me a gift. She gave me a feeling I never had in my whole life.

I came down here to write something but I can't do it.

And:

I think about the baby all the time. I can't help it. I can't help it.

And:

Nothing. Nothing. I want to tear out the paper and rip it into pieces.

And then he came to the part he'd read over and over again, trying to distill from it the certainty he'd lived with most of his life:

My son hates me. I see it in his eyes. Last night something bad happened. I was talking to Clarice in her room. She is unhappy. She is sad all the time. I was trying to find out what was wrong, but she wouldn't talk. I tried holding her like I used to when she was little. She is not a little girl anymore. She is almost a woman. God forgive me for the feelings I had when I held her in my arms. I couldn't help myself. But I didn't do anything. I didn't do anything but hold her. She never cried. Never said a word. I left. When I came out of her room the boy was standing there. His eyes were accusing me. I almost hit him. I never hit my children, but I wanted to beat the crap out of him. From the day he was born, the second I held him he would cry.

His eyes stung with tears. He didn't know if they were tears of pity or of hate. He stood up, held the notebook like a baseball pitcher, and threw it as hard as he could. It skidded across the floor and stopped at the wall under the poster of Alfred E. Newman.

Chapter 11

Later that night Daniel ran the events of the afternoon He had spent hours in libraries obsessively reading sources on the subject of incest. There were more than a few theories about causes: stress in the family, drinking, a need for a nurturing figure, etc. One that got his attention was a study that centered on a poor relationship between the husband and wife. Because there was little or no affection, the result was usually infrequent or non-existent sex. In this kind of situation, the husband often turned to the eldest daughter to provide what was missing.

He had never seen any affection between his father and mother, so according to that theory, it was more than possible his father could have turned his attention to his daughter, Clarice.

He stared at the notebook spread out on the gray floor. He picked it up, sat down, and opened it once more.

Rumors are flying around the factory that F. had a baby. How do these things start? Nobody knows who the father is. But that doesn't stop people from guessing. They name everybody from Mr. Knudsen to Blackie. I don't talk about it with anybody. Meanwhile I am waiting. I promised I would help her but I haven't seen her or heard from her in months. Not since before she left the factory. I think about her. I want to see her, touch her. I want to see the baby. I think about finding where she is but I know if I ask any questions I will give myself away. I wonder if the baby looks like me. I don't know if it is a boy or a girl. I even dream about F. We go to that Italian restaurant. We have dinner. We drink wine. Sometimes in the dream, I try to hold her, but I never do, something always stops me.

A letter. One of the girls from assembly walks past me on a break and shoves an envelope into my hand when nobody is looking. I put it in my lunch pail. I knew right away who it was from. I read it in the car on the way home. After I read it I hid it under the seat under a bunch of rags. It was a short letter but nice. She tells me she is fine, the baby is fine. It is a girl. Her name is Angelina. She says I can send money to a post office box she set up. Whatever I want to send she says will be appreciated. Thanks a lot. No mention if I will ever see her or the baby. She makes it pretty plain they are out of my life. And I am out of their life. All she wants now is money. But I promised. So I will send it.

When I send her money I write asking to see her, to see the baby. She never answers. I look for the girl in the factory who gave me the letter. I see her but I don't know what to say. She might know but she might not know. I think about waiting to get her alone, but then what? I write again. This time I beg. Please let me see the baby. Still no answer. I threaten to stop sending money, but it makes no difference. She knows her Max. She knows that when I make a promise it is good as gold.

Alex turned to the next page. There was nothing on it. He went on for several more. He remembered they were blank as well. He let the pages run against his thumb. He went through them, searching for what he had seen before.

Towards the end, perhaps the fourth or fifth page from the back, there they were, the words on the page, letters tilting in all directions as if they were bowing before a force of nature. They were on the lines, above and below the lines, in large letters and small letters, in script and in block print; some of the letters were straight, some were backward, and some were tipped forward. All the words were the same word. It was as if he were practicing how to write the word in every manner possible. The single word was, "Angelina."

Chapter 12

Alex read the notebook again and again. He skipped pages. He went back and forth, rummaging through it like a scavenger in an attic full of memories. He had never before grasped what should have been obvious: that his father was more than just the man he had hated all his life. His father was a person, another fucking human being with the flaws and character traits and emotions and desires that other ordinary human beings had. He could not believe it, but he was beginning to feel a certain amount of sympathy for the old man.

ↄ৩৫৩

Clarice was his protector. When he was little and their father made him cry, she was there to hold him. "I won't let him hurt you," she said. And when he got older and would not cry but would get angry instead, she would calm him. "Don't get upset. It's not worth it. He doesn't hate you. It's just that he likes girls better."

Chapter 13

When Alex finally left the basement he found the house dark. He turned on a light and looked at his watch. It was almost midnight. He carried the notebook upstairs and found Miriam in bed holding a book and watching *Nightline* on TV. He put the book on top of the dresser.

"Are you finally done with it?" She wore a sleeveless nightgown—she was never cold—which left her shoulders bare. Her glasses were sitting on the end of her nose. Her eyes above them, gray with flecks of blue, were not as cold as they had been for quite a long time. The button at the neck of her nightgown was open, revealing the top of her full breasts, a reminder of their ability to arouse him.

He nodded. "Finally."

"Before I forget," she said. "Richard called today. He's in a play. It opens next week."

"Off-Broadway?"

"More like Off Off Off-Broadway. It's on Avenue B. He invited us to the premier."

"Premier. You make it sound like they're going to have klieg lights and celebrities."

"Give him a break. He's got to start somewhere."

"Sure. I just can't help feeling that they're going to eat him alive. He's too soft, too sweet."

"You never know. He might surprise you."

"They're going to swallow him and spit him out on the sidewalk."

"He's got plenty of resilience."

"He'll need it."

"You're going to be there, aren't you?"

He took off his shirt and loosened his belt. "There's that tone in your voice."

"I just asked a simple question."

"I'll never be forgiven for missing the school play in eighth grade."

"I didn't say a word."

"You said it all then." He stepped out of his pants and reached under the pillow for his pajamas. "Anyhow, I'll be there. You can count on it."

"Good."

He was on his way to the bathroom when Miriam said, "Would you mind if I read the diary now?"

He got it from the dresser and handed it to her. "Knock yourself out."

The next morning he felt hungover. He had a headache and a foul taste in his mouth. He showered and dressed and went downstairs to find Miriam having breakfast.

"There's coffee," she said.

"Thanks." He filled a mug and sipped it slowly. Some mornings the first cup of coffee was something to be grateful for.

"I was up a long time after you fell asleep," she said.

"I was out in two seconds, I think."

"I couldn't stop reading. I read most of it twice. And what he had to say about you must have hurt like hell."

"It did," he said. "But I was no prize, either. He treated me like shit and I gave it right back to him."

"I saw that thing about Clarice. He swears he didn't do anything to her," she said.

"I know what he says. But what do you believe?"

"Honestly, I can't say."

"Can't or won't?" he asked.

"Why would I lie to you? If I thought what he wrote proved anything I'd tell you."

"Okay, I can see I'll never convince you," he said. "So let me ask you something else. What do you think I ought to do about my newfound sister?"

"What do you mean, *do* about her?"

"Like try and find her."

Miriam set her cup down. "You've got to be kidding, right?"

"I'm not kidding. You think it's such an outrageous idea?"

"My first thought is, it's insane."

"Why? What's so nuts about it? I find out I have a sister. Isn't it natural to want to locate her?"

"I don't think so." Shaking her head. "Not after so many years."

"What do the years have to do with it?"

"Look, I know you're all shook up over this. And I don't blame you. I would be, too. But there are a million questions. How do you find her? And if you do, what do you tell her? The truth? Does she want to know? Will she thank you or shoot you? All kinds of things like that."

"People are found all the time," he said. "I'm just thinking off the top of my head. I could hire a detective. A private eye."

"You're not serious, are you?"

He had no answer. For whatever reason, everything that was going on suddenly seemed bizarre. He and Miriam, talking together as if nothing had ever happened between them. Here they were, living in the same house as a married couple, in the same bed every night for more than a year where their only touch was accidental. It was like being in a theater of the absurd, like they were actors on a stage, playing at being a couple.

"I don't know," he finally managed to say. He knew he was equivocating and despised himself for it. "Maybe I am serious."

Chapter 14

The funeral home had been in Rockville Centre, not far from where they lived. It was a square, brick building that occupied the entire block.

The day of his father's funeral they had entered through double glass doors. The lobby was carpeted in a dark patterned broadloom. To the side of the entrance was a discreet signboard with white plastic letters on a black background containing the names of the dead and the rooms in which they were to be found. Alex had seen his father's name listed there as if he were one of the speakers at a convention: Gunther, Max…2B.

They had found the room, coffin at the back, polished oak, and bronze fittings. Part of the cover was hinged back, revealing the upper half of the body. A soft light beamed down on the coffin, bathing it in an eerie glow.

There was only one person in the room when they arrived. A stranger to Alex. He was a short man with a round face, the skin of which had as many creases and folds as a bloodhound. His eyes were blue dots. "I worked with Max in the same shop. Before he retired. He was a good tool and die man. Very good. I worked with him for years." He glanced at the coffin. "I saw the obituary in the papers. I am sorry."

"Thank you," Alex said.

"Very kind of you," his mother added.

"For what? I pay my respects to an old friend. For that, I don't need thanks."

The man went over to the coffin and stood with his hands clasped behind his back.

Alex followed and forced himself to look at his dead father. He saw the lightly rouged cheeks, the gray hair neatly parted on the left, the thin nose, the once hard mouth now soft, closed for good. He ought to feel something. There should be some grittiness in the eyeballs, at least. A dryness in the throat. It was his father, after all. A bubble had exploded in his father's brain and he was dead. He could not repress the heave that came up from his stomach, burning his throat, gagging him.

Now, almost two weeks later, he tried to remember the man's name. What was it? It would come to him he was sure, but if not, his mother might remember, or it might be in the guest book they always gave you in funeral parlors. If he had written his name, he would probably have also written his address, in which case there would be no problem locating him. But after he found him what would he learn? That was one question. And what other questions would he ask? And what if there were no answers to his other questions?

He called his mother.

"Rudi Emmenthaler," she said immediately.

Rudi, a friendly, familiar kind of name. "I wasn't sure you'd remember."

"I wouldn't have, except he sent me a sympathy card."

"Is his return address on the envelope?"

"I don't know. I may have thrown it out. What do you want it for?"

"Would you look?" His mother threw out things almost as fast as she got them. Leftovers, clothes, and souvenirs were disposed of before they had a chance to become memories.

"Just a minute." He heard the phone being put down, only a moment later she was back. "It was on my desk. I still have to send him a thank you card."

"Is there an address?"

She read it to him, someplace in Brooklyn, a number on East 31st Street. It meant nothing; he didn't know Brooklyn. "Thanks, Ma."

"What do you want it for?" she asked again.

He hesitated, "I thought I'd talk to him. He said he was a friend of Dad's. Maybe he knows something."

There was a long silence. "This has to do with the diary?"

"Yes."

"Alex, I don't think that's a good idea."

"Why not? You read it. You must realize I have a sister out there somewhere."

"So that's what this is all about?"

"I don't even know myself what it's all about. I just have this feeling that I want to know more."

"I think you should let it rest."

"I don't think I can. Besides, why should I?"

"Lots of reasons. So many reasons. I can't even begin to tell you."

"Give me one."

She sighed. "For a start, it can't help but open old wounds. Don't you see that?"

"Then why did you let me know about the diary in the first place? Why did you give it to me? You were the one who said I should read it."

"You know what? I shouldn't have. I made a mistake. I thought you…" He could hear her voice break. "I thought you would learn something about your father. That he was not a monster. That he was a decent man. Even though he had an affair he was still a decent man." She was clearly crying now.

"Mom, Mom. Please don't. I'm not trying to upset you."

"Then tell me you won't do this."

"I can't tell you that."

"I didn't expect anything like this to happen."

"I'm sorry. But I lost one sister and now I know I have another one. How can I just forget about that?"

She sighed. "I was never able to change your mind about anything before. I'd be foolish to think I could do it now."

"I'm not trying to hurt you, Mom."

"I know, Alex. I know. But I still wish you wouldn't do this. It can't lead to anything good. At least tell me you'll give it some thought before you go ahead. At least promise me that."

"Okay, Mom. I'll think about it. I promise."

Chapter 15

Miriam wondered what Alex was going to say when she reminded him it was the night they were going to dinner at her mother's house.

He surprised her. "I completely forgot, but no problem. Just let me wash up and change. Do you know anything about the guy she's seeing?"

"I know his name is Henry Mancini."

"The composer?"

"I wish. But no, just the same name."

"What does he do?"

"He's apparently a good dancer and a smooth talker. That's about all I know."

In the car they drove without speaking. Miri glanced sideways at Alex. He was still good-looking, strong jawline, a straight nose, no wrinkles. She blamed herself in part for letting things deteriorate to where they were now. But Alex had his share of responsibility, as well. He'd been distant for a long time, his mind always off somewhere. The discovery of his father's diary seemed to have made everything worse, magnifying all the inconsistencies, the tension between them, spinning their relationship out like an elongated strand of a spider's web. In the past, their sex life, which had always been strong, provided a bond when stress drove them apart. But for quite a while now that part of their marriage had disappeared, just as their closeness, their unstated intimacy had also vanished. Among other things, she'd considered the possibility that he was having an affair, but each time she began thinking about what was happening to their marriage, she'd eventually push all her thoughts aside. She'd briefly considered the possibility of having an affair, herself. She'd once had a flirtation with her old boss, but it had been only that, a flirtation. There was no one now who might be a candidate, nor, in truth, was she really interested.

What was more worrisome, and hard to put out of her mind, was what had happened that morning. A few days earlier, she'd gone to her gynecologist for her annual checkup. Before she'd left for work, a call had come from Dr. Patel's nurse asking her to come in. She'd driven to the office aware that something had to be wrong.

"What is it?" she asked.

"Please sit down, Miriam."

She sat on the edge of the chair, hands clutching her purse.

Dr. Patel said, "The radiologist saw something in your mammogram. But it was not clear. It could be nothing. We both agreed however, that it should be followed up."

"What does that mean? What's the next step?"

"The next step is to see a breast surgeon. He will look at the pictures and decide whatever is appropriate. The important thing is to identify exactly what is going in your breast."

Miriam felt the air go out of her lungs. She closed her eyes and managed to take a breath, "You think it's cancer?"

"Now don't get ahead of yourself. I didn't say it's cancer. I don't know what it is. But it's important to find out. I'm going to have my nurse make an appointment for you with Dr. Bromley at Long Island Jewish. He's one of the best."

She'd left the office feeling numb. The appointment had been made for the following Monday. She'd sat in her car for a long time. Should she tell anyone? Alex? Her mother? Richard? She knew she would have told her best friend, Eve. They'd been friends since elementary school, but Eve had gone and gotten herself killed in an automobile accident when she was barely thirty years old. Richard was out of the question. He had enough on his plate. Mabel? How could she do that to her when she'd just found someone to make her happy? That left Alex. Of course, he'd say and do all the right things. But would he really mean them? She didn't think she could bear it if she thought he was just doing what was expected of him. In the event, she decided that for the moment, she would keep this news to herself.

Alex turned off the Belt Parkway in Brooklyn, at Flatbush Avenue. They'd be at her mother's apartment house in ten or fifteen minutes. Her mother hadn't gone out with anyone since her father died fifteen years before. Why the need for a man now? But why was she thinking like a Victorian prude? *My mother is still young, the juices are probably still flowing. Why shouldn't she have some fun? Maybe I'm upset because I'm not having any fun.* At any rate, she hoped the man her mother was seeing would turn out to be a good guy, not some full-blown jerk.

Her mother lived in an apartment house on Ocean Avenue near Cortelyou Road. That section of Ocean Avenue consisted of six-story apartment houses that had been built thirty and forty years before. It was a middle-class neighborhood, so most of the buildings, although old, were kept in decent condition. There wasn't a doorman, but the lobby was furnished with a table and a few chairs and had a marble floor that gleamed with fresh wax. The elevator was clean, although it rattled somewhat as it took them to the fifth floor.

Her mother greeted them at the door wearing her gypsy look—dark makeup, purple pajama pants, a matching silk blouse, layered with necklaces, dangling earrings, and bracelets up and down one arm. "Come in, come in. You're late. We've been waiting forever."

"It takes a long time to get to Brooklyn," Miriam said. "And besides, we're not late. You said, seven o'clock, and—" she looked at her wrist "—it's exactly seven."

"Never mind. I forgive you." She turned to Alex. "I'm so sorry about your father, dear. Now come in and meet Henry."

Waiting for them with an air of expectancy was a short, stocky man holding a glass in one hand, while the other casually nested in the pocket of his gold-buttoned navy-blue blazer. He wore a gray silk turtleneck, tasseled loafers, and had a pencil mustache and teeth so white Miriam knew they had to be bleached or dentures. He put down his glass.

"So you're Goldilocks," he said, enveloping Miriam's hand between both of his. "Your mother didn't lie. She said you were beautiful." He squeezed her hand and leaned forward to kiss her on the lips but she avoided that by giving him her cheek. He then turned to Alex, shaking his hand vigorously. "What can I get you guys to drink? I'm playing bartender tonight."

"Red wine," said Miriam.

"You sure you don't want something stronger?" her mother asked. "Henry makes a fantastic margarita."

"My press agent," said Henry.

"Wine will be fine," Miriam said.

"Wine will be fine," Henry repeated. "A poet and you don't know it."

"I'll try the margarita," Alex said.

"You got it."

"Come in, come in," her mother said, arms fluttering as

if she were shooing in a gaggle of geese. "Sit down and make yourselves comfortable."

A narrow table in the living room had been set up as a bar with bottles, glasses, and a blender already filled with Henry's specialty. On the coffee table, accompanied by a stack of small dishes, were hors d'oeuvres—pâté, crackers, a wedge of Jarlsberg, goat cheese, brie, guacamole, crudités, and a bowl of mixed nuts.

Miriam looked at the array and said, "My God, Mom. There are only four of us. This spread is enough for an army." When she saw the look of dismay on her mother's face she wanted to cry. What was the matter with her?

"I thought you'd like something to snack on."

"I'm sorry. I don't know why I said that. The food looks wonderful."

Henry, hand poised above the blender, said, "Hold on a few seconds, folks." Everyone looked at him as he made a show of switching on the machine. It made a clattering sound like a helicopter hovering over the roof. They froze in place as if they were children playing *Red Light Green Light.* After what seemed like much more than a few seconds, he turned it off. "I had to warn you. It makes a lot of noise because I got ice in it. But it's a concoction worth waiting for. Taste it and see."

He poured the foamy liquid into stem glasses and gave the first one to Mabel. "For Madame, the hostess with the mostess, and not the firstest one she's had tonight, I might add." Then a wine glass to Miriam, and lastly, "For us boys."

He held up his glass. "How about a toast? Know any good ones? The only ones I know can't be repeated in mixed company."

"How about, thank God we're still here?" Miriam said.

"Miriam!" Mabel said, "What kind of a thing is that to say? Your grandfather always said, 'Good health and a long life.'"

"I'll drink to both of those," Alex said and took a sip of his margarita. "Umm," he said. "This is very good, Henry. Really good. Maybe the best I've ever had."

Miriam scowled at him, angry with herself for her outburst.

"Thanks. I am pretty good at making drinks if I do say so myself."

"Oh?" Miriam said. "How come?"

"When I was a kid, I used to tend bar after school. To make a buck, you know?"

"And what were you studying in school?"

"How to survive."

"What school was that?"

Henry reached into the bowl of nuts and popped some into his mouth. "The school of hard knocks. Ever hear of that one? Ha ha."

"Funny," said Miriam. "But what do you do, for a living, I mean?"

"I don't do anything. I'm retired." He put his glass down and cut a piece of the brie, putting it on a cracker. He held it out, "Anyone?"

Alex reached for it.

"I meant when you were working," Miriam said. There was an edge in her voice and she knew it, but couldn't stop herself.

"Henry was in insurance," her mother said. "Weren't you, Henry?"

Henry smiled. "Mabel darling, I can speak for myself. Your daughter wants to quiz me, that's okay. I understand. She wants my bonafides, wants to protect her mother. I respect that."

"Whoa," Alex said. He took another piece of cheese. "It's nothing like that. Miriam's a curious person, that's all."

"I don't need defending," Miriam said. "I'm sorry I asked. It's really none of my business. I was just making conversation. It's not important. Not important at all."

"Hey! Don't back off now. Keep pushing. I like that," Henry said.

Mabel said, "Have some of these hors d'oeuvres. I don't want to have too many left over."

"The cheese is delicious," Alex said.

Henry smiled, took a long drink from his glass, and patted his lips with the back of his hand. "I'm happy to answer Goldilock's question. To be honest with you I did a lot of things. I was a shoe salesman. I sold appliances. I worked for E. J. Korvette a long time. Then I decided to go into insurance. Whole life. It's a great business. Each sale pays off for at least seven years. It's like the energizer bunny, keeps going and going."

"See?" her mother said. "Plain and simple. Now, what do you say about dinner? Anybody hungry?"

When they were seated at the table, her mother said, "I made lasagna. With Henry's help, of course."

Henry shrugged. "What can you do? I like to cook. That's all there is to it."

Dinner went smoothly, considering. Alex looked attentive and smiled at whatever Henry had to say, but Miriam could see his mind was elsewhere. The lasagna turned out to be exceptionally good, so it wasn't too difficult for Miriam to make the appropriate comments. She hoped it would make up for her earlier gaffe. Throughout all, her mother's smile was everlasting. Miriam found this disconcerting because it was so unlike what she was used to from Mabel.

Before coffee and dessert, she helped clear away the dishes. When they were alone in the kitchen, her mother closed the door, then said, "Well?"

"Well, what?"

"Well, what do you think?"

"Of Henry?"

"No, the milkman. Of course, Henry. Isn't he charming?"

"Another Cary Grant. Just shorter."

"Don't be flippant. I really like this man. I want you to like him."

"Why do I have to like him? *I'm* not going out with him."

"You mean you don't like him?"

"I didn't say that. He seems very nice. Just…"

"Just what? What don't you like?"

"I didn't say I don't like anything. It's just…"

"There's *just* again. What's the just?"

"He doesn't seem to be…your type."

Her mother took a step back. Her eyelids fluttered. Then she laughed. "Oh, I get it. I know what it is. He's too low class for you. Right? Not somebody you'd lend money to. Is that it?"

"Did you lend him money?"

"A little. He needed it to cover his rent. It's no big deal."

"How much did you lend him?"

"Not that it's any of your business…two-hundred dollars. Not worth making a fuss about."

"I'm not making a fuss about it. Did you hear me say anything?"

"I can see the disapproval in your eyes," her mother said.

"Well, it doesn't strike me as a great start to a relationship for one party to be asking the other for a loan."

"That's not the only thing that's bothering you, right?"

"Now you mention it…"

"Of course. I know why you look down on him. It's because you're a snob. That's what you are, you know.

Ever since you went to college. A snob. You look down on people who don't have a college education."

"That's not true," Miriam said. "It has nothing to do with education. But maybe you're right. Maybe I am looking down at him a little." She took some dishes over to the sink and began to rinse them. How could she tell her mother she didn't really give a shit about that schmuck, Henry? What if what she had turned out to be cancer? Dying at the age of forty-one? That wouldn't be so great. "I'm sorry. I'm just not in a good mood. I don't mean to spoil anything."

Suddenly, without warning, she felt tears come into her eyes. Her shoulders shook as she began to cry.

Her mother put an arm around her. "You're crying."

"I know."

"You never cry. You never cried even when you were little and fell down and hurt yourself."

"I'm not little anymore, in case you haven't noticed." Miriam tore off a paper towel and dabbed at her eyes.

"So what's going on? You and Alex having problems?"

"What makes you think that?" Miriam was glad had mother had raised this. It allowed her to keep the cancer possibility to herself.

"I wasn't born yesterday. I notice things."

"Oh, you notice things." Miriam sat at the small table in the kitchen. "So what did you notice? That we don't talk to each other anymore? That we don't communicate? That we haven't had sex in I don't know how long?"

"It's that bad, is it?" Her mother sat down next to her. "My poor baby. I had a feeling something not good was going on. But I didn't want to stick my nose in. You know I don't do stuff like that."

"I know, Mom. It's just as well. If you tried, I probably would have bitten your head off. I was going to tell you about it last week, that day we had lunch, but I just couldn't."

"Poor baby. What're you going to do?"

Miriam shook her head. "Alex and I are going to talk. That's what we said on our way over here. What good it'll do, I don't know."

"I think you'll work it out. It's been a solid marriage, hasn't it?"

"I thought so. But something's shifted, and I don't know what it is." Miriam stood up. "Let's get back. They're probably wondering what happened to us. How's my face? Did my mascara run."

"A little." Her mother put a napkin under the faucet, then patted Miriam's face with it. "Fine. Beautiful as ever. Are you ready for dessert? Henry made a lemon meringue pie."

დოდ

On the way home, Miriam had a fleeting thought that she would tell Alex about the doctor in order to see his reaction. Instead, she made small talk about Henry and the evening. Alex listened and grunted in response. When she told him about the loan, he laughed. "The guy's a character, all right. But I wouldn't worry. I don't see him taking your mother for all she's got."

"I'm not so sure about that," Miriam said. "She's in love. Women do strange things when they love someone."

Alex turned and looked at her. "So do men," he said.

Chapter 16

Weekends were difficult. Alex was home. All day, both days. Miriam was at her shop on Saturday, so for her, that was the easier of the two. She also knew that Alex usually did chores on Saturday while Sunday was all day football. The chore he'd told her he was going to do was redo the grout around the bathtub. That, and his watching unending football helped her get through it.

On Sunday, after their breakfast of bagels and lox, they settled down in the living room with the Times. Alex put a record on. She heard Louis Armstrong's raspy voice singing, *"Come to the cabaret, my friends, come to the cabaret."* She wasn't a fan of that kind of music, but today it didn't matter because she barely heard it. She looked at the newspaper but couldn't get herself to get through an article. The breast doctor…Alex…tell him or not…Alex…what to do about their relationship. She knew it was important to talk about it. But why couldn't Alex bring it up? Why should it be up to her to do anything? Because that's the way Alex was. Most of the time he was passive, almost always letting her make decisions about their lives, from buying furniture to what movie to go to. That was why she was surprised that he was talking about looking for his sister. Maybe she should have encouraged him, instead of telling him it wasn't a good idea.

Monday arrived, the day she was seeing the surgeon. She was having coffee with a slice of toast when Alex came into the kitchen. He poured a cup and sat down opposite her. She looked at him for a moment, then before she knew what she was doing, she threw the piece of toast at him. "So unless I bring it up you're never going to say a word. Is that it?"

He put his hands above his head as if in surrender "What's this about?"

"I'll tell you what this is about. Since we don't talk and we don't touch, maybe we should start thinking about a divorce. That's what this is about."

"Is that right? So it's all my fault?"

"It doesn't matter whose fault it is," she said. "I'm sick and tired. I'm sick and tired of the whole situation. We should be talking about us, about our problems. But you won't. All you think about is your father. That damned diary. Your dead sister. Your new sister. Essentially, all you think about is yourself."

He put his cup down hard, spilling coffee. "Maybe you're right. Maybe we should get a divorce."

She fought to keep the tears back. "Go to hell!"

Chapter 17

He'd spent the entire day thinking about what Miriam had said. She'd shaken him up, no doubt about that. Was that her intention, or did she really want a divorce? He hated the idea of it. For some reason, he'd always considered divorce a dirty word. He didn't know where that came from. It certainly wasn't his parents' marriage, one that he'd considered more an unemotional contract rather than a marriage. Divorce meant failure. It meant giving up, admitting that you'd screwed up something very important. He felt that he and Miriam had had a good life. He knew he wasn't wrong about that. They'd had some wonderful times together. They'd produced a beautiful son whom they both loved. But he acknowledged that in the past year their relationship had changed. The intimacy they'd shared had vanished. He had felt himself withdrawing from her. It never used to bother him that she made all the decisions, but now it did. He felt she was bossing him around. It made him feel like a wimp. So why didn't he say anything? Why did he keep his annoyance hidden instead of bringing it out in the open? Maybe he was a wimp, or maybe he was just trying to avoid confrontation, to avoid scenes like the one this morning. He knew he ought to sit down with her and discuss their marriage. Perhaps they should see a marriage counselor. If he suggested it, she might be willing. But maybe it was already too late.

At the end of the workday, he was tired, confused, and felt another headache coming on. He was sure of only one thing, he did not want to go home. The idea of facing Miriam and trying to deal with all that was going on was just too much for him to handle. You're a miserable coward and a weakling, he told himself. But if he wasn't going home he needed to call. It wouldn't be fair to have Miriam waiting for him, not knowing where he was.

He picked up the phone and dialed the number at her store. His stomach was wobbly when she answered the phone.

"Hi," he said. He spoke in a low voice, not wanting anyone to overhear.

"Hi yourself."

"I wanted to let you know I won't be home for dinner. Something's come up here. I have to work late. I'll grab a bite in the city."

"Fine."

He hesitated. There was dead air between them.

"Is that all?" she finally said.

"Yes."

She hung up the phone.

Now that he'd done it, he was somewhat relieved. He looked across the office at Wanda. He didn't allow himself to hesitate. He wrote a note asking her to stay in the city with him for dinner, clipped it to some papers, and put it face down on her desk. "Take a look at these," he said, in an all-business voice. "It's important."

She gave no indication whether she agreed to do as he asked. He left the office last and headed towards the newsstand two blocks away where he said they should meet. He wondered for a moment whether he'd done something stupid. Miriam had mentioned divorce. Did he want that? Was this the first step toward adultery? Then he saw

Wanda, facing away from him. He felt a rush of pleasure he hadn't experienced in a long time. Traffic was already backing up from the Holland Tunnel, the cars fretting and honking as if they were cattle on the way to the slaughterhouse. The sidewalk was filled with moving bodies but Wanda stood out as if she were spotlighted on a darkened stage. She wore an amber-colored jacket with wide shoulder pads, a man-tailored style she favored.

She turned towards him and he could see the whiteness of her neck framed by her hair. When he reached her, on impulse, he put his arms around her. Before she could say anything, he kissed her. When she didn't resist he tentatively explored her mouth with his tongue. She responded, entwining her tongue with his.

When they broke apart Alex said, "Just like the movies."

"Like a soap opera if someone saw us."

"A lot of people saw us, my darling girl. Didn't you hear the applause? That was my best Rhett Butler imitation."

"Are you cracking up?"

"Probably. Come on. I've got a lot to tell you."

They walked in the direction of Chinatown. She put her arm through his, and occasionally as they walked, he felt the softness of her breast pressing against him. "I didn't even ask. Do you feel like Chinese?"

"I love Chinese food."

He hadn't known that. But why would he? He didn't know much about her. He knew she was divorced, had a daughter, Judy, in her first year in college. And, of course, a mother who had just been diagnosed with cancer. Was there a father? He wasn't sure if she had ever mentioned her father. He knew nothing about her ex-husband.

The sidewalks in Chinatown were clogged with people. Walking was like playing dodgeball. The stores never seemed to close, except for the banks, and who knew if they weren't working behind closed doors? The windows of the shops were filled with ivory Buddhas, painted bamboo fans, jade jewelry, and other tchotchkes. Food stalls sold strange vegetables. Unfamiliar odors came out of fish stores and butchers whose windows had ducks strung up like decoys that had been stripped of paint. They passed a wedding in progress, saw congregants lighting candles through the open doors of a Buddhist Temple.

"How's your mother doing?" he asked.

"Okay, I guess. They're going to start treatments soon."

He didn't pursue it. He felt it was morbid and upsetting to ask the questions everyone asked: How far had it spread? Were they doing chemo or radiation? How was it being tolerated? He thought he still had the old attitude that even a mention of the Big C. would bring doom upon the person uttering it as well as upon those hearing it. When Aunt Bessie was dying, he was sent out of the room whenever they talked about her illness.

His favorite restaurant of the moment was a storefront on Pell Street. It held about forty people, mostly Chinese. The only English spoken was unintelligible and the menu was only in Chinese. The place was family-run—a mother, father, and two elderly men, probably relatives. What he liked was they were too busy to smile at him and treat him as if he were a wonderful round-eye doing them the honor of eating in their establishment. It was more that they tolerated his being there as well as his stupidity for not understanding their language.

He ordered by looking at what was on other tables and pointing at what looked good, or else by pointing at the menu, hunching up his shoulders and holding his hand's palms outward in a pleading manner, hoping this would get him something good. Mostly, it worked.

He watched her maneuver a dumpling into her mouth

with chopsticks. "Listen…I didn't tell you this before, I don't know why I didn't…I guess I just didn't want to get into it…"

"Tell me what?" she said.

"About my father. He kept a diary. My mother found it and gave it to me to read. And—" he stopped.

"And?"

"It's complicated. I don't know where to start."

"You mean maybe you still don't want to get into it. It's okay. You don't have to." She reached for another dumpling.

"It's not that. It's…complicated like I said. It has to do with my sister. I told you about her."

"Yes. I know you still miss her."

"Exactly. That's part of what's bugging me. It seems my father had an affair. The woman got pregnant. There was a baby. A girl. So it means I have another sister somewhere."

"Wow. That's some kind of news."

"I was playing with the idea of trying to find her. What do you think about that?"

She held up a hand. "Hold on. Back up a little. Give me a minute to digest all of this."

One of the elderly relatives brought a platter of vegetables. Steam and a smell of ginger floated upwards. Alongside it, he placed another platter and two more bottles of beer. Alex saw pieces of something floating in a brownish liquid. He had no idea what it was.

Wanda drank from the bottle. Alex liked to pour his into a glass and watch it foam. "Let me ask again. What do you think about my trying to find this woman who's my sister? I want your opinion. It's important to me," he said.

"Who else have you asked?"

"My mother. She's dead set against it. Thinks it's a bad idea."

"Why is that?"

"Thinks it'll open up a can of worms."

"What about your wife? Didn't you ask her?"

"Also against it."

"What's her reason?"

He paused to think. "The woman, if I find her, might be devastated. I think that's what she was saying."

"They may both be right. But this person out there is, after all, your sister."

"You think I should do it?"

"If that's your gut feeling, sure. Everything depends on how strongly you feel about it."

"I'm not sure myself," he said. "I'll have to think about it more."

Wanda used her chopsticks to take something from the unknown plate. She held it up. "What is this?"

"Not a clue," he said.

She popped it into her mouth and chewed. "Well, it tastes good, anyway."

"I'm glad," he said. "And I think you are a very smart lady. I also think it might be possible to fall in love with you."

Wanda's response was a tight smile. "That wouldn't be a good idea."

"Probably not."

"I'm not kidding," she said. "I like you. I'd like to go to bed with you. But that's it. No ties. No commitments."

"You know exactly what you want, don't you?"

"I guess so."

"Do you really believe you can stick to ideas like that? Things happen. Sometimes they happen even though you don't want them to happen."

She didn't answer. After a while, Wanda put down her chopsticks and patted her mouth with her paper napkin. "I've had it."

"Me, too. There's a lot left. You might as well take it home."

"I don't feel like carrying a paper bag full of leftovers," she said.

"How about if I carry it?"

"All the way to my place? Is that what I think you mean?"

"That's exactly what I mean."

"How will that play at home?"

It came out with surprising glibness as if he'd been rehearsing it all day. "I've been thinking about getting a divorce."

Chapter 18

He felt strange as if time had stopped as if they were alone at a table somewhere in a place without walls, the light a photo flash, everything frozen into stillness. Then sound intruded, voices of people talking, laughter. They were still in the restaurant, still across from each other.

Wanda's head swiveled toward him, her eyes showing points of yellow like a cat. "Wait a minute."

"I didn't know I was going to say that."

"Why did you? You never once even hinted at it."

"Things have been happening at home. Not good things."

"Let's get this straight," Wanda said. "What did I just say? No ties. No commitments. First, you talk about love. Now divorce." She shook her head, the movement causing her hair to cover one eye. She brushed it away. "The last thing I want to do is break up a family."

"What if it's already broken up?"

"I don't know about that." She held her napkin tight and began twisting it. "Look. I think maybe we're going too fast here. I'm not ready for this."

"Wait a minute, I'm not asking you to do anything. I'm not trying to pressure you." He reached across and touched her hand. "Let's just see how it goes."

Outside, they decided on a cab to Penn Station. They

began walking toward Canal Street where there was the best chance of finding one.

He held the bag of leftovers in one hand and reached to take her hand with the other, then abruptly, changed his mind. Coming towards him was the suddenly familiar and now unwelcome sight of his son. He only at this moment realized how stupid it was of him to have brought her to Chinatown. Richard lived fewer than a dozen blocks away.

"That's my son ahead of us," he said.

"Isn't that nice," Wanda said.

They stopped and waited. Alex watched his son's face go through a cycle of surprise, puzzlement, and eventually, understanding.

"Dad. This is a surprise."

He held out his hand and Alex gripped it. Richard's hand was larger than his, as was the rest of him, and the handshake was a crushing one. Richard worked out in a gym because he believed a fit body might help his career. "You never know when they might want me to take my clothes off for a part." And indeed, if it were only physical attributes that were required, his son would already be a star. Alex was in awe of how his and Miriam's somewhat ordinary genes had intermingled to produce in Richard the looks of a supermodel. Health, vitality, and charm seemed to flow out of him in a tidal wave.

"My son, Richard," Alex said to Wanda. Then to Richard, "This is Wanda Folsenlogen. She works in my office."

Richard shook Wanda's hand.

Alex tried to sound casual. "Wanda and I just had dinner together." Then he added, "We were working late."

"That sounds nice," Richard said. "As a matter of fact, it's my night off. I'm meeting my roommates over at The Chin Palace. Do you know it? Big portions and cheap."

"No," Alex said.

Richard shared an apartment with two others. One was

a young, strikingly handsome black man, whose name was JaMarcus Young. He had ferociously white teeth and a nose, mouth, and chin that looked as if they'd been stolen from a Greek statue. The other was an Asian girl who called herself Li Ling. She was tall, very thin, hair cut short like a boy's. When Alex first met her she had on a black body stocking, with a loose white sweatshirt over it, thick black eyeliner, and bright patches of color on her cheeks which made her look like a beautiful marionette. They made a dramatic trio.

Richard acted unconcerned and unaware of his father's distress. He reached into the pocket of his jeans and came out with several pieces of paper. "You know I'm opening Friday night, don't you? Mom said you were coming, right?" He separated one of the papers and handed it to Wanda. "This is a flyer we made up. Why don't you come too, Miss Folsenlogen? It's a terrific play. You'd enjoy it."

"Thanks," Wanda said. "I'd love to. But I'm busy this Friday."

"Too bad." Richard shook hands with her again. "Listen, I've got to go. I'm late. Nice meeting you." Then he looked at his father, not smiling now, the contours of his face hardening like cement. "See you." He walked away from them with long strides.

"Why do I feel like shit?" Alex asked.

"Because your son caught you with another woman."

"We were having dinner. What's wrong with that?"

"Don't be silly. He thinks you're fucking me."

They began walking again. They did not touch. When a taxi stopped for them, they sat apart from each other.

"Your son is gorgeous." She looked at the flyer Richard had given her. "What kind of a play is it, '*Iago's Dance of Death*?'"

"No idea. But you know these avant-garde theater groups. It could be a comedy."

"Is he any good?"

"I don't know. The only thing I ever saw him do was high school stuff. There was no way to tell. Not that I'd necessarily know, anyway."

They rode farther in silence. Then Alex said, "I think he's gay." He had always been aware of femininity in his son, who had preferred putting on his mother's lipstick and earrings, wearing her clothes and high heels, to playing with cars and train sets. He had tried not to let it disturb him, but it had. The ultimate irony, of course, was that his father had always thought of him the same way.

"There are worse things," Wanda said.

"Actually, I don't care if he's gay. I don't mean that. I do care. I don't want him to be gay. But I can live with it. Only I'm afraid for him. It's dangerous."

"Life is dangerous."

"Sure it is. You can get mugged anywhere but if you drop into Central Park at 2 AM you're asking for it."

They didn't speak again until they got to Penn Station. Then Alex said, "I think we ought to take a rain check on tonight, don't you?" He held out the bag from the restaurant.

"You keep it," she said, turning to leave. "I hate leftovers."

He waited until she got on the train, then dropped the food into a trashcan.

Chapter 19

The surgeon's office was in a medical building on Union Turnpike, not far from Long Island Jewish Hospital. Like every medical building Miriam had ever been in there was a faint smell of antiseptic as well as an atmosphere of dread. The information board noted that the doctor's office was on the second floor. She took the elevator and walked along a seemingly endless corridor. She heard strange sounds and imagined they were the buzzing of x-ray machines, or dentist's drills, or people's souls crying in agony.

In the office two women sat behind a glass enclosure. One of them slid the window open. She didn't smile or greet her, just asked her name, and told her to sign in. When she did she was handed a clipboard.

"Please fill out the forms and bring them back to the desk."

She didn't expect to be treated like a long-lost friend but the abrupt manner of the woman made her even more uncomfortable than she already was.

She filled out three pages of questions about insurance, medications, privacy, why she was there, and who had sent her. She had to put her name and address at the top of every page. By the time she was finished, she was irritated and tired even though it was only nine o'clock in the morning. She brought the clipboard back to the desk and asked how long it would be before she saw the doctor.

"It won't be long," the woman said, not looking at her. She had a face that was shaped like a plum, with tiny pouty lips. Miriam repressed the desire to lean over the counter and rake her nails across that little plum face.

There were several rows of chairs, and a table with a pile of magazines to help pass the time. She had no desire to read any of them but picked up a copy of Harper's Bazaar anyway.

She turned the pages of the magazine but the words didn't register. She remembered her mother taking her to the dentist when she was a little girl. There was a waiting room like this one with benches and hard chairs and magazines on a table and a few toys for children to play with. Every few minutes she looked at the clock on the wall above the receptionist's window. Its second hand ticked as if it were stuck and had to drag itself around the surface of the clock. After an hour had passed she was about ready to scream.

She thought once again about her father. These thoughts would come intermittently, at random. He was a shadow. She was not quite five years old when he died. All she remembered of him was a smell of aftershave and pipe tobacco. She didn't remember his voice. She had no clear vision of his face, although there were photographs of him. When she looked at the photos his picture could have been of anyone, an uncle, a friend. What she often felt in these thoughts was a yearning for something impossible, a father who told her he loved her.

She told herself it would do no good to get upset about waiting. That's what you did in doctor's offices. They didn't give a damn about the patients who were kept waiting for hours just to have a word with the great man.

She got up and went to the window again. The glass slid open and plum face looked up at her.

"How long will it be? My appointment was for nine o'clock. I've been waiting over an hour now."

"Doctor is just finishing with his patient. You'll be next." As Miriam turned away, she said, "You may go in now. I'm sorry you had to wait so long."

Now Miriam felt guilty for having hated her. "Thanks."

Dr. Bromley smiled and shook her hand. He was a stocky man with thinning blond hair. He picked up a folder from his desk and glanced through it. "I see the radiologist couldn't confirm what it was he saw, even though he did a sonogram, as well. But don't worry, we'll find out what's going on." He sat at his desk. "Let me tell you what we're going to do. First, I need you to give me your medical history and your family's. Then I'll examine you. And after that, there'll be a full physical checkup. Okay?" Without waiting for an answer, he said, "Let's begin."

She went through all she could remember of her own medical history. There wasn't much: the usual childhood diseases—tonsils, measles, an appendix removed. Her father had died of heart failure. As far as she knew her mother had never had anything seriously wrong with her. There were no siblings.

She changed into a gown. He listened to her heart, and lungs, poked her stomach, kneaded her band ck, palpated her breasts. He made notes but said nothing. A nurse called her into another room, weighed her, took blood pressure, drew blood, told her she could get dressed, and then go back to the doctor's office at the rear.

After she sat down, he said, "Here's the story so far."

She held her breath.

"I can't feel anything in your breasts, so I'm going to have to do a biopsy. It's a surgical procedure, quite simple, nothing to worry about, but it has to be done in the hospital. You'll be an outpatient. You won't have to stay overnight. We'll send the tissue I remove to the lab. That's when we'll find out whether it's benign or whether it's cancerous. Any questions?"

She stared at him, noticing for the first time that his eyes were a pale gray, with almost no color at all. Her throat was so dry she couldn't swallow. "May I have a glass of water?"

"Of course." There was a sink in his office. He filled a cup and gave it to her. "I understand that you're upset. It's only natural. But at this stage, you have just as good a chance of it not being cancer as it is of being cancerous. The odds are actually in your favor, based on your history. It's very possible that it's simply a slight calcification."

She tried to smile. "I'll try and hold that thought."

"Good. See the nurse at the desk outside. She'll make an appointment for the surgery. It will be sometime next week."

She sat in her car in the parking lot. Why me? she thought. Then got angry with herself. Why not me? Don't be such a crybaby. Stop feeling sorry for yourself.

For the first time in years, she wished she had a cigarette.

Chapter 20

There was Wanda and there was Miriam. A lot to think about. Maybe too much. In addition, Alex still couldn't get the thought of a sister out of his mind. He decided to make an exploratory phone call to his father's friend, rationalizing that it didn't invalidate the promise he'd made to his mother not to pursue his idea.

A woman answered, a husky voice, scratchy, a smoker's voice.

"Is Rudi Emmenthaler there?"

"Who is this?" the voice demanded as if he were breaking a rule of some kind.

"My name is Alex Gunther. My father was an old friend of his."

"Just a minute."

The phone was put down. A long time seemed to pass. He could not hear anything. Maybe the old man had been asleep and she was waking him. At last he heard a scraping noise and then his father's friend came on the line.

"Hello? Hello? Who is this please?"

"Rudi?"

"Yes. Who is speaking?"

"It's Alex Gunther. You remember? Max Gunther's son? You came to the funeral."

"Oh yes. I was not sure my wife got it right. I am surprised to hear from you."

"I'm a little surprised to be calling. But something turned up. I wanted to ask you a few questions."

"What about?"

"Well, I'm not sure how to begin. It's about my father. It seems he kept a diary."

There was silence. "He what?"

"Kept a diary. And there's a lot in it." He paused, uncertain now how to proceed.

There was no help from the other end.

"I can't go into the whole thing right now. It's a little complicated on the phone."

"So why are you calling?"

The Germanic literalness at work, he thought. "Maybe I could come over and see you. I could explain it better in person."

"No," Rudi said, at once. "That would not be possible. My wife is not well. We are not having visitors."

"I'm sorry."

"Yes. It is a difficulty." There was a pause. "I must go now."

"Maybe I can call another time?"

"The situation will not change."

The phone clicked.

Damn! It was so quick. He thought he should have said more, kept him talking. But he hadn't wanted to bring up intimate details on the phone.

He'd called from the office at the end of the day. Later, when he was home after work, he thought, what the hell was there to be afraid of? So many years had passed, what difference would it make now?

He decided to call again but didn't want to do it in front of Miriam. He didn't want to have to explain what he was doing and why he was doing it. After dinner, she turned on the TV. He went upstairs and called Rudi from the bedroom.

"Bear with me Mr. Emmenthaler. Just let me tell you this. In the diary my father mentions a girl in the factory. He got involved with her. There was a child…" He paused, waiting for a reaction.

After a moment, Emmenthaler said, "How do you know this?"

"Because my father wrote it. He says he had an affair with this girl and she had a child. But he never saw it. The child's name was Angelina."

"I do not believe this," Rudi said.

"I didn't believe it myself when I first read it. But it's there, in his own handwriting."

"Max actually wrote this down? Everything?"

"Not everything. He didn't write down the name of the girl. That's why I'm calling. I want to find her. I was hoping you might know."

"I don't know. How would I know?"

"There were rumors going around. I thought maybe you heard something."

"No. This is all new to me."

"Are you sure, Mr. Emmenthaler. You don't remember anything? A single girl…pregnant…in those days? People must have been talking."

"I do not know anything about any woman, or any baby. This was more than thirty years ago. And you expect me to remember? I can tell you for sure one thing. Max never said a word to me. Not a word."

"Wait a minute. Maybe this'll help. The woman's name begins with F. The initial, F."

"It means nothing to me. I did not know any of the factory girls. I worked in the machine shop. I minded my own business. I am sorry."

The interview was over. Disappointment. He had hoped to get some information, anticipated he would be at least a little closer to finding his sister. "Okay, Mr. Emmenthaler, thanks anyway. I hope your wife is better."

"Thank you."

"Sorry to bother you."

"No bother."

Chapter 21

The appointment for the biopsy was now only a couple of days away. How many hours? No matter how hard she tried Miriam couldn't stop thinking about it. She went to work hoping contact with people would distract her, but it didn't. She had stomach cramps. Her eyes were dry. Artificial tears helped somewhat. While speaking to customers or her salespeople, she was nagged by other thoughts. She felt that the people who loved her would want to know and it was important for them to share her burden. With the exception of Richard, not telling anyone was essentially a selfish act. She was still too upset with Alex to tell him. That left only one person.

She called from the small office in the back of her store. "Mom, I've got something to tell you."

"Uh oh, sounds ominous."

"It may be, in fact. I might have breast cancer."

"Oh my god, Miriam." Her mother's voice rose in pitch, almost to a squeal. "You're not serious. When did this happen?"

Miriam told her about the annual checkup and the visit to the breast surgeon.

"So what's next?"

"I have an appointment Monday. They're going to do a biopsy."

"Where are you?"

"I'm at work. In my store."

"I'm coming over. I'll be there in an hour."

"Mom. You don't have to do that. I'm okay. Really I am."

"Sure you are. You're a tough cookie. I know that. But I'm coming over anyway."

An hour later she was there. No yucks, no smart remarks. She walked over to Miriam and put her arms around her. "You are my daughter and I love you. You know that, don't you?"

"Yes. I know that."

"Let's go out for a cup of coffee."

"Mom, I've got customers."

"I know, but you've got help."

Miriam had two employees, one full-time and one part-time. "We're just going out for a few minutes. Won't be long."

There was a bakery a few blocks away that had small tables and served coffee. After they'd gotten their coffee, Mabel said, "You've been having a rough time."

"You might say that."

"Have you told Alex?"

"Not yet."

"Because?" When Miriam didn't answer, she said, "I guess it's for the same reason you didn't tell me."

"No," Miriam said, looking down at her cup. "Not at all. At first, I didn't tell anyone because I thought the whole thing was insane. That it would just go away. That the doctor would tell me it was all a mistake. Like a bad movie where they find out it was someone else's x-ray. In this case, a mammogram. But that never happened, of course. And then I didn't want to worry you. With Alex, it's entirely different. I know I'm going to have to tell him, but I just couldn't do it yet."

"What about Richard?"

"He doesn't need to know."

"I'm not sure I agree, but that's your decision. I'm sorry about you and Alex. I always liked him." Her mother reached across the table and covered her hand, giving it a squeeze. "But don't you worry. We're in this together now. I know you're going to beat this thing. We'll show them whose boss."

"Thanks. I feel so much better, now that I've told you."

"Sure you do. It's hard to keep something like that inside. Now think about telling Alex. No matter how many problems you have between you, he deserves to know."

"Yes. I suppose he does. By the way, this coming Friday is Richard's opening. You're going to come, aren't you?"

"Of course. Henry and I are planning on it. Now tell me the date and time of your appointment and exactly where it is. I'm going with you."

Miriam felt tears come into her eyes. "I love you, Mom."

Chapter 22

The phone call to Rudi disturbed him. He couldn't understand why there seemed to be so much hostility from the guy. Then, abruptly, the thought of Rudi triggered something his mother had said when she'd told him about the diary. Letters. He'd been so obsessed with the diary he'd forgotten about the letters.

"Yes," she said with a sigh when he called. "I was hoping you might have forgotten about them."

"I did. But then I remembered. I'll come over tomorrow and get them."

He went the next day. He brushed his mother's cheek with his lips. As usual, she was fully made up. The air in the house had a chemical smell. They went into the kitchen where he recognized the smell as Clorox. His mother had a fear of germs and always used the bleach on the countertops as a deterrent.

There was a plastic bag on the table. She frowned as she gave it to him but said nothing.

When he got home he found a tin cookie box in the bag his mother had given him. He pried off the cover with the gold writing that spelled out, *Hans Christian Andersen Danish Butter Cookies.* The lettering encircled a picture of a bearded man wearing a tall hat, riding a goat, and holding a dead bird in his hand as if it were a prize. He wondered what that had to do with cookies.

In the box were letters still in their envelopes, not many, maybe seven or eight, and some postcards, the addresses written in childish script, his own and Clarice's. He opened one of his, curious, and reading his own words of how proud he was to have ridden a horse tumbled him back to his childhood. He remembered that day, the nervousness but also the excitement of getting on the animal's back. He fingered Clarice's letters, touched them with his fingers, but then saw a plain white envelope without a stamp that made him drop the ones from Clarice. "Max" was written on it. There were two letters in the same envelope, written in an open circular script, the pen steady and sure of itself. They were not dated. He withdrew the letters hoping they were from the woman who had borne his father's child.

Dear Max,

Money received and much appreciated. You are a kind man. I am living on my own now. It is not easy but the baby makes it all worth it. She is so beautiful. Thanks for telling your friend. He also offers help without asking for anything in return. You are both good people. I am sorry if I hurt you.

There was no signature.
The second letter was a little longer.

Dear Max,

I thought you would want to know that I had a baby girl.
Grazzy D. Remember my pigeon eyetalian for Thank God? She weighed 6 pounds 8 ounces when she was born. She is healthy and cute and has brown hair. I named her Angelina on account of I think of her as an angel from Heaven. My folks were good to me, I am still at home with them but am leaving soon. Grazzy D again. I could use the

money you promised me. Whatever you send will be ap-
preciated. You can send it to PO Box 780, General Post
Office, NYC. Don't worry about me, I will be OK. I hope
you are OK too.

He had read the letters in reverse order. But the message
was clear. What friend was she talking about? The only
friend he was aware of was Rudi, who had said he didn't
know anything. Or was there some other friend in those
days that nobody knew about?

He got his father's diary and opened it.

...F. told me she is pregnant...I have denied God...

How did the old man feel when he read those letters?
How did his mother feel when she read them?

Alex looked up. He was in the kitchen where he had
installed a new faucet, hung the ceiling fan, painted the
cabinets. At one time these chores had given him comfort,
a feeling of satisfaction, but no longer. Miriam was in the
den, probably doing her record keeping.

...She's not in the shop anymore...
...Maybe she can find somebody...give the baby a fa-
ther...

He closed the notebook and read the letters again. Rudi
Emmenthaler. He tried to remember the conversation. He
had said he knew nothing. Was he a little too emphatic?
Was he too quick to cut short the conversation, as if he
might have had something to hide? Of course, the man's
wife was sick. That could certainly have something to do
with not wanting to waste his time on the phone with some
kook asking questions about the distant past. And besides,
why would he lie?

He took the letters and went into the den to show them to Miriam. As he'd expected, she was at her desk. "Look at these," he said. "Tell me what you think."

She read them, then re-read them. "I'm not sure what you want me to say."

"As far as anyone knows my father had one friend if you can call him a friend. This guy Rudi Emmenthaler, who came to the funeral. I called him. He said my father never told him anything. Nothing about a girl. Nothing about a baby. So who is this friend who offers help? Don't you think it's got to be him?"

"I don't know. Why would he lie?"

"That's just what I asked myself. I have no clue."

"Well, I guess it's possible," Miriam said. "Maybe this man, Rudi, helped them to meet, covered up for your father. Maybe your father would tell your mother he was going someplace with this guy, you know, or something like that."

"You think? But why would he lie about it?"

"Could be embarrassed. Wouldn't you be? Tell your friend's son you were helping his father cheat on his mother?"

"Yeah, maybe you've got something there. That does make sense." He put the letters back into the envelope. "And you know what? I can't shake the feeling he knows more than he said."

"Even if he does, there's not much you can do about it."

"I don't know. Maybe I could go and see him. Confront him with the actual diary. It might shake him up enough so if he was lying he might decide to tell me the truth."

"Whatever that is."

"Right," he said. "Whatever that is."

He began to leave when Miriam said, "Alex, wait a minute." She turned in her chair to face him.

He stopped. She looked down at her hands then up

again. She pressed her lips together and began to twist the silver bracelet on her wrist. "What is it?"

"I'm not sure how to tell you this."

"I have a bit of a health problem."

"What do you mean, health problem? Can you be a little more specific?"

"All right, if it's specificity you want." She took a deep breath. "I may have breast cancer."

Alex stared at her, taking in what had just been said. He began to speak but something caught in his throat. He gulped air, and finally managed to say, "I'm sorry." He immediately realized how woefully inadequate his response was. "I don't mean that. No, of course, I'm sorry. When did you find out? How advanced is it?"

"I don't know if it's advanced. I'm not sure if I even have it. They're doing a biopsy to find out."

He pulled a chair over to her desk and sat down. "You've known about this for some time, haven't you?"

She nodded.

"I don't have to ask why you didn't tell me. I understand. And I don't blame you one bit." He shook his head. "I'm such a putz. Here I am obsessing about the past and you're confronting something much more important."

Miriam said nothing, but her eyes filled.

"When are you having the biopsy?"

Her voice was barely a whisper now. "Monday."

"Tomorrow?"

"Yes."

"Would you mind if I was there?"

"No, I wouldn't mind. I'd be glad if you came. My Mom is coming, too."

"What about Richard?"

She shook her head. "I don't want him to know."

"Why not? He's your son. He deserves to know, doesn't he?"

"You don't understand. I wasn't going to tell anybody. I was going to be the great heroine and deal with it by myself. It was only today I told my mother. And now I'm telling you. But Richard...no." She put her hands over her eyes. "He doesn't have to share in this. He has enough problems just trying to survive in New York."

"Okay. I won't argue with you." He looked at her. She was holding herself, making an effort not to cry. He wanted so much to reach out and touch her but held back. "I don't know what to say, Miriam. I wish I could do something to make all of this go away."

"So do I," she said.

Chapter 23

They had gone to bed without any more discussion of the biopsy. Miriam was on her side of the bed, Alex on his. It still surprised her that in the same bed where they'd often cuddled and held each other as well as made love, they now managed to sleep without ever touching. It probably helped that it was a king-sized bed.

Alex was asleep. She could hear the steady rhythm of his breathing. She was not only awake but fully alert, eyes open, staring up into the darkness. She desperately wanted to sleep but her mind was as if it was on the Cyclone, the roller coaster she'd gone on with her friend Ellen when they were kids. They'd screamed as the car threw them upwards, sideways, and made their stomachs lurch when it dropped. Her memories came at her the same way, speeding upwards on one memory and then racing downward with another. She tried to shut them off by using various tricks she'd read about. One was to concentrate on her body beginning with the toes, then move up through each part: the instep, the shinbone, the knee, and so on. First one leg, then the other. The idea was that if you concentrated hard enough your mind would shut down sufficiently for you to fall asleep. She couldn't make it past her thigh before her brain was off and running again.

Next, she went back to the old standby of counting sheep jumping over a fence. Forget that one. She tried different sleeping positions, first lying on her right side. A few minutes later she turned on the other side. She lay face down with her left arm up and her right under her. Then she switched arms. She felt her breasts and wondered whether she would still have them after this was all over. What would she look like?

Nothing stopped the flood of memories. Astounding memories. Scenes from childhood, friends, old school-teachers, people she hadn't seen or thought of in years. Other memories were so confusing she knew she must be dreaming because she found herself in caves, or climbing a mountain.

Then came a clear one. She was in the bookstore where she'd first met Alex. What was the name? She stared upwards trying to remember. The *Strand*. That was it. She'd seen him on the other side of the table where she'd been browsing. He looked up at that moment, their eyes met, and something happened. A rush of heat to her face. She never blushed so it surprised her. It was then she decided to pick him up.

She crossed over and stood next to him. He was holding a book, *The Magic Mountain* by Thomas Mann. She could sense he was aware of her presence.

"I've never heard of that book," she said.

"I've read it twice," he said as if they were continuing a conversation. "It's terrific."

That was how it began. On their first official date, he brought her a copy for a present. She'd never told him her opinion of it. She'd never finished it.

The memory brought tears to her eyes. This made her berate herself. *Stop being so sentimental. It was a long time ago. He's not the same person and neither are you.*

Before Alex there had been others. She'd lost her virginity at sixteen with a boy she'd met at the roller-skating rink she went to with Ellen. Shelley was older and quite

smooth. She and Ellen were skating together when he
caught up with her and asked if she wanted to skate one
turn with him. He was fun and asked her out. He had a car
and drove her to a make-out place in Canarsie. When it got
hot he reached down and touched her. She let him. She and
Ellen had talked about what it would be like and now was
an opportunity to find out. When he suggested she take off
her panties, she didn't hesitate. He climbed on top of her,
thrust a couple of times and groaned. Afterward she told
Ellen all about it. She also wouldn't be seeing Shelley
again.

"Why not?" Ellen said.

"At first I thought he was cute. But when it was over he
just zipped up and drove me home without saying another
word. He was just so damned pleased with himself. Not a
thought about me. I was another notch on his belt, another
score. Just wait till he calls me again."

"What're you going to do?"

"I'm going to tell him to get lost. Maybe hint that he
wasn't that good a lover. That should shake him up a bit,
don't you think?"

The sex got better and more enjoyable. There was one
boy with whom she became really serious. She was in college then and they talked about marriage. He brought her
home to meet his family. She could tell right away his
mother wanted no part of her, a poor girl with a widowed
mother. It wasn't long before they broke up. He began to
weep when he told her his mother wouldn't allow it. Miriam was deeply hurt but still felt sorry for him. Every once
in a while she would think about those days and wonder
what her life would have been like with Jason.

She'd eventually fallen asleep but it had not been rest-
ful. The alarm woke her. Her eyes and her body ached
when she got out of bed.

She showered, dressed, and went downstairs to find

Alex waiting for her.

"Want some breakfast? I made coffee," he said.

"They told me not to eat anything."

"Of course, I forgot. Then let's go."

When they arrived at the hospital, her mother was already there, wearing her usual assortment of necklaces and bracelets, and fully made up. A surprise was that Henry was with her. He was wearing the same blazer and turtleneck he'd worn the night of the dinner. The men shook hands, the women kissed cheeks and they went inside.

Miriam went through the admitting process and was directed to the surgical floor. The others were told they could go to the waiting room where they would be notified when the procedure was over. She wondered if she'd done the right thing not telling Richard. But it was too late now.

A smiling young woman wearing green scrubs greeted her at the nurses' desk. She took Miriam into a small room with two beds. Neither bed was occupied. She handed Miriam a hospital gown and told her she could change in the bathroom.

People came into the room and attached tubes to her. An anesthesiologist spoke to her. She didn't quite register what he was saying. She did her best to smile and nod her head as if she understood everything. After some time she was taken out of the room, still on the same bed, and was wheeled along a corridor. She looked up at the fluorescent lights in the ceiling. She felt the rolling movement of the bed and with peripheral vision was aware of other people in the corridor. For some reason, it seemed as if she were dreaming again.

They took her into the operating room. Nurses in scrubs and masks looked down at her. She heard them telling her all was good and it would soon be over.

The next thing she knew was waking up in the recovery room. Her head felt heavy, and her eyes ached. She touched her breast and felt bandages. Her other breast was intact, thank God. Her eyes closed and she fell asleep again.

She woke up to see Dr. Bromley at her side.

He opened her gown, examined the bandages, and covered her. "It went well. I've already spoken to your family. I don't want to get your hopes up, but I will say I'm optimistic. We should have the results within a week. At that time I should be able to remove the stitches. In the meantime go home and rest."

Sometime later her mother came in with Alex. Henry did not join them. She was glad of that and guessed her mother had something to do with it. When she felt strong enough, Alex left and her mother helped her get dressed.

"Would you like me to go home with you? I could make dinner for you and Alex."

"I don't think so, Mom. I doubt I'm going to be hungry. I'll probably have some tea and toast."

"I can handle that," Alex said.

After they'd said their goodbyes, and were on their way home, Miriam dozed again, waking up when they stopped. In attempting to get out of the car she became dizzy and almost fell. Alex was able to catch her. He had his arms around her and held her close until she said, "I'm all right now." When he let go of her she had a fleeting moment of regret. It had felt good.

Chapter 24

The next morning Miriam assured Alex that he could go to work, that she was perfectly capable of being by herself. "I won't be doing anything but resting anyway," she said.

"You're sure?"

"Absolutely."

Almost immediately, Rudi Emmenthaler was again in the forefront of his mind. He put his father's diary along with the letters in an old attaché case and took it with him to the office. There was no proof, just a gut feeling he had that Rudi was holding something back. He knew the only way to find the answers was to see him in person. He put the case in one of the drawers of his desk and began to work. But in a short while he found he couldn't function. His mind was still so preoccupied with Miriam as well as what he was going to say to Rudi and what Rudi might answer that he didn't hear what anyone said to him. "What?" he found himself saying again and again. The papers he looked at were incomprehensible. When he was on the phone he would realize in the middle of a conversation that he had forgotten who he was talking to. There was no way he could wait until the end of the day to see Rudi.

Stuart Roth was in his private office with the door closed. Alex felt that he kept the door closed to give the impression he was hard at work. What he was usually doing was chatting up buyers and arranging lunch dates. Alex had to admit he was good at that. Those lunches often transformed into heavy duty orders.

He knocked on Roth's door and went in. As expected, Roth was on the phone.

He held the phone with his right hand and showed the palm of his left to Alex while continuing his conversation: "So how does that sound? Tomorrow, one o'clock. Smith and Wollensky." He listened to the other person responding, then said, "Hey, some red meat once in a while is good for you. Okay, then." He put the phone back on its cradle. "They love those steaks when they don't have to pay for them. What's on your mind?"

"I have to go out."

"So go out. Since when do you need my permission?"

"I wanted you to know because I'm not sure if I'll be back."

"Again? You just took a day off." Roth leaned back in his chair. It was one of those high-backed leather chairs that swiveled and rocked. "What is it with you lately, Alex? You don't seem to be your old self. It's like you're not here even when you're here. Know what I mean?"

"I have a lot of things on my mind."

"I understand. I guess your father's death shook you up quite a bit. It's something I personally went through myself, so I understand. But you got to get hold of yourself. We got that union thing going on. I know they're talking to our guys. They're hitting every non-union shop down here. I told you before, it's up to you to head them off at the pass. Get on the case, man. Now if you have to go somewhere, go ahead. But come back and take care of business. If the union gets in we may all be out of a job. Understand what I mean? I don't want anything unpleasant to happen."

Alex did not answer. He understood quite well what

Roth was getting at. But the threat passed through his nervous system without causing so much as a tremor. He didn't give a shit about Roth or his job. What kind of a job was it anyway? Assistant to the master of bullshit? He should have left a long time ago. But that was another story. He couldn't think about that now. He walked slowly out of the room closing the door carefully behind him, retrieved the attaché case, and left the office.

He took the subway to Brooklyn. He had bought a Hagstrom's map, which showed all the streets in all the boroughs. With that, and questioning Ruthie who lived in Brooklyn, he had worked out how to get there. He got off at the Kings Highway station. There was a bus he could take that stopped not far from Rudi's house.

The block Rudi lived on in Brooklyn could have been the one where Alex grew up in Valley Stream, except the houses on the Brooklyn street were attached, so there were twice as many. Now they would be called "townhouses." Other than that, it was the same: neat, postage-stamp lawns, hedges trimmed into squares, chain link fencing.

He found the number he was looking for and went up a full flight of brick steps to the front door which was to his right, and a cement porch freshly painted dark maroon to his left. The front door had an oval top and was painted the same color as the cement. A screen door had to be pulled open to get at the doorbell. He held the attaché case in both hands and was suddenly assailed by doubts. Why was he here? Was he doing the right thing to bother these people? Did they deserve his raking over the past? Yes, he told himself. He had to find out. He pressed the doorbell and once again he heard the familiar chimes of his childhood. When he was growing up every house he'd ever been to had chimes, their sound producing a gaiety that must have been as artificial to those inside as it was to those outside.

The door was pulled back and a small woman was

standing in front of him, young and old at the same time. Her skin was the color of weather-faded wood, which had the effect of emphasizing her painted lips. Her eyes were dark stones partially concealed behind oversized eyeglasses with a red frame perched on the end of her nose. A printed cloth was wrapped turban-style around her head. Her body seemed too small for the elegant outfit she wore as if she were a child playing grown-up. She did not say anything, but her expression had the passive hostility of someone waiting to hear the pitch of a door-to-door salesman.

"Yes? What is it?"

"I'm not selling anything," he said.

"I've heard that before." Her voice was the husky voice he had previously heard on the phone.

"No, really. I'm looking for Rudi Emmenthaler. Is this the right house?"

"It might be." She looked him over with a myopic stare. "Who are you?"

"My name is Gunther. Alex Gunther. I spoke to you on the phone a few days ago."

"This is the right house. What are you doing here?"

"I came to see Rudi."

"Did he know you were coming?"

"No. But it's important I see him."

She hesitated a moment as if deciding what to do, then stepped back. "Come in then."

He walked into a small living room.

"Sit down. I'll go get him." She went past him and disappeared behind a door.

He did not sit. He was not calm enough. His stomach rumbled. He did not know what he was going to say to Rudi. He should have rehearsed it, should have thought about it more, maybe talked it out with Miriam. She would have known what to say, what questions to ask.

The room smelled musty as if windows had never been opened. It had a couch covered in beige linen, two uphol-stered chairs, a coffee table with a heavy book on it, *English Gardens*. The walls were painted the color of egg-shells. On a cabinet were several framed photographs. He went closer to get a better look. There was one of Rudi and his wife when they were much younger. She was pregnant. It was clear the photograph had been taken in the photog-rapher's studio. There was a false background of trees and an arbor. The two of them were smiling but it was the kind of smile you get when the photographer asks for it. Not quite real. Another was with Rudi's wife, now holding a baby. Once again she was smiling, but this time it was gen-uine a happy smile. In the third photograph ,the couple were posed, holding hands with a little girl about six, all of them smiling for the camera.

Rudi came through the door at the other end of the din-ing room, followed by his wife. In contrast to her silky brown pants and beige and brown tweed sweater which were too big, Rudi wore a white shirt too small for him, buttoned to the neck, no tie. His pants were work chinos, the kind night watchmen wore.

"Mr. Gunther," Rudi said, coldly, but he held out his hand.

He shook Rudi's hand. He felt the calluses rough against his own softer hand. "Please call me Alex."

Rudi gestured. "Sit, sit."

Alex sat on the edge of one of the chairs and put his hands on his knees. Rudi's wife sat at one corner of the couch facing him, Rudi stood at her side, his right hand on her shoulder. Alex cleared his throat. "I was just looking at those pictures. I hope you don't mind."

"Of course not," his wife said.

Alex saw Rudi's left hand tighten briefly into a fist. He cleared his throat again. "Listen, uh, could I ask a favor?

This is difficult for me."

"What?" Rudi asked.

"I hope you won't be insulted, Mrs. Emmenthaler, but could I speak to Rudi alone? It's kind of personal."

She stood up quickly. He had the impression she was glad to leave them. "I don't mind. I have things to do, anyway."

"You're sure you don't mind, Liebchen?"

"No." She touched Rudi's cheek. "You and Mr. Gunther do what you have to do." She went up the stairs to the second floor.

"I asked you not to come here," Rudi said.

"I know. But this is important."

"My wife is ill."

"I'm sorry," Alex said. "I don't mean to upset anybody." He had determined to be calm, and assertive, without getting excited. He laid the attaché case on the coffee table, opened it, took out the notebook and the envelope with the letters. "This is it. This is the diary I told you about."

Rudi glanced at it, then at Alex.

"You remember we talked about the diary?"

"Of course."

"Since then, I came across a couple of letters, too."

Rudi said nothing.

"Do you want to see them?"

"No. Why should I?"

"The letters are from the girl he had the baby with. In one of them, she talks about a friend of my father's who is helping her."

"What does that have to do with me?"

"I thought maybe you were that friend since I think you were the only friend he had."

"I don't know about that. Maybe there were others. All I know is that I did my work. After work, I had a beer with your father. I went home."

"Would you take a look at the letters please?"

"What for? What good would it do?"

"You're telling me you never heard any of the rumors? You didn't notice anything? My father never said anything?"

"Sure I noticed. Your father was moody a lot. But it did not mean anything special to me."

"You know what I think? Forgive me for saying this, but I think you're not telling the truth. I don't know why, but I can feel it."

"You're calling me a liar? In my own house?"

"I'm not calling you anything. But it says right in here…" He could hear his voice rising. He took the letters out of the envelope and flattened them open. "Look at this. Look what it says." He held the letters in one hand, the one he wanted to show on top, and pointed with the forefinger of the other hand as if he were in a classroom, "…*Thanks for telling your friend. He also offers help without asking for anything in return. You are both good people.* That's not you she's talking about?"

Rudi shook his head.

"Who is it then?" He heard his own voice, loud, insistent. "Who is it if it isn't you?"

Rudi's wife came partly down the stairs. "Why are you shouting? What's going on?"

"Go back upstairs, Francesca," Rudi said. "This is between us."

She continued down and came over to where they were now both standing. "Why are you shouting at my husband?"

"I'm sorry," Mrs. Emmenthaler. I didn't mean to yell. But Rudi is keeping something from me. Look at this." He held the letters out. "Get him to tell me the truth."

Francesca looked at the letters, then at her husband.

The old man inclined his head toward them. "Just a minute. I need my glasses."

"You don't need your glasses," she said.

Alex saw Francesca look at Rudi and saw Rudi shake his head slowly from side to side and then suddenly it was clear to him who Francesca was. *The diary...of course, the woman with the initial F...*He felt a kind of thrill at the revelation. He'd actually discovered something.

"Don't—" Rudi said.

"These things have a way of coming out, don't they?" She sighed, and said to Alex, "It's true. You're right. Rudi knew. Your father confided in him."

"And you?" Alex stared at her, trying to see her as the young woman in the photograph he had looked at.

"I'm the girl who wrote those letters." She smiled. "At least I was a girl then."

"So that's how it was."

"Yes. Rudi helped me. He never asked anything of me." She took Rudi's hand in hers. "I don't know what I would have done without him."

"Liebchen..." Rudi said.

"But why did you cut my father out? He said he loved you. He wanted you and the baby, didn't he?"

"I didn't want to break up a family. He had a wife and two children."

"I know. I was one of them."

Francesca sighed. "Try to understand. I admired him. He was a good man."

"If he was so good, why did you hurt him like that?"

"There was no other way. Can't you see that? Is what I did so terrible?"

"I'm sorry. I had no right to say such a thing. I'm sure there was plenty of hurt for everybody."

Rudi put his arm around his wife and led her to the couch. Her breathing was rapid and shallow, her eyes red-rimmed. "I think you should go," he said.

"You don't understand. I came here to get help in finding my sister."

A wail, like the cry of a waterfowl, came out of Francesca's mouth. "No…no…you can't…"

"Why not? I lost one sister. She died a long time ago. Now I have a chance to find another one."

"No."

"I need to find her. Try to understand. It's very important to me."

"Important to *you*! What about to *her*? She doesn't know anything about this. Rudi is her father. That's what she knows."

"She's not a child. She must be what, thirty-five, forty years old. She can handle the truth."

"Why should she? If you told her about this you'd be turning her life upside down. Why should I let that happen?"

"I think I have a right to know her."

"No," Rudi said, moving over to stand in front of him. "You don't have any right. You don't even have the right to be here. I want you to go."

"This is not your call, Rudi."

"This is my house. I want you to get out. Now."

"Francesca," Alex turned to her. "Francesca, listen to me. I'm her brother. Even though I'm a half-brother, shouldn't she know she has one? Wouldn't it be good for her to know this?"

"No," Francesca said, not looking at him. "Absolutely not. She knows enough. She doesn't need to know any more."

Rudi's posture changed. It looked as if he was about to attack Alex. "Go now," he said.

"You shouldn't do this. She'd want to know me if she knew I existed."

"What is she missing?" Rudi said. "Are you such a wonderful person? I don't see such a wonderful person. You come uninvited to my house. Order me around. Make my wife cry. She's very sick, for God's sake. She has enough problems. You think we need more from you?"

He heard what Rudi said. His wife wore a turban, her skin was gray, she probably had cancer. He understood it, but he could not stop now. "Just tell me what I want to know and I'll go. I'll get out of your hair. That's all I want. Her name. Where she lives. I won't just barge in on her. I'll break it to her gently."

"No…no…" Francesca whispered. "Leave her alone."

"You heard what she said." Rudi gestured toward the door. "Get out. Or I call the police."

Alex felt sorry for her illness, sorry for bringing back a past they would rather forget. At the same time he felt a terrible need to know. There was so much he didn't know. Why had Clarice abandoned him? He'd always felt it was somehow partly his fault. And Miriam. Was she going to have cancer too? Would she end up looking like Rudi's wife? What had driven his father into this woman's arms? He paced back and forth, his mind a jumble of conflicting thoughts. Then he had an idea. "Please. Give me a photograph of her, at least. How about that?"

Francesca's cheeks were wet with tears, her arms wrapped tightly about herself.

"I will give you nothing," Rudi said. "Now leave us in peace."

Alex rubbed his eyes, and bowed his head. It was as though the blood running through his veins had become thick as oil, and was now moving like sludge. If only he had been able to get them to understand. For all he'd learned he really hadn't accomplished anything. He'd been a Don Quixote tilting at windmills. All he'd managed to do was cause pain and hurt to these innocent people.

He was suddenly very tired. It was an effort to reach down and pick up the diary and the letters. Somehow, he managed to get them back into the attaché case. Then he straightened up, holding the case in one hand. It felt heavy now. He had to hold it with both hands.

"I'm sorry," he said. "I wish it hadn't come to this. I don't know what else to say."

And with that, he found himself moving, heading towards the front door. He pulled it open and without looking back, walked out of their house, closing the door softly, but firmly behind him.

Chapter 25

Alex stood on the sidewalk in front of Rudi's house. He couldn't move. His legs were trembling. He tried to breathe deeply to calm himself. He had gotten here by bus but could not remember from which direction he had come. In that quiet neighborhood, he doubted there would be any taxis. He stood there for some time before he felt able to walk.

His legs were still unsteady. A woman came towards him with a small dog on a leash, a mutt of some kind, but with a cute little tail that stuck up like an antenna. The dog came over to him, pushed against his leg, and looked up with doleful eyes, begging to be petted. He held the attaché case in one hand and reached down with the other to stroke the soft fur of the dog's head.

"Don't mind her," the woman said.

"It's okay," he said. "I like dogs."

As he continued his walk, his body began returning to normal. It also no longer seemed to him that he had wasted his time, but he could not help acknowledging that he had caused Rudi and Francesca a lot of pain. He came to a bus stop and waited, but when no bus arrived after twenty minutes he began to walk again. He did not know exactly where he was but he guessed he was heading in more or less the right direction to get to the subway.

When he had walked about a dozen blocks he came to

a street of stores. He went into a deli for a container of coffee. It was busy with the lunch crowd. He watched people order sandwiches, soups, and salads, any one of which he would gladly have eaten on an ordinary day. But this day was not ordinary. He had no appetite. He swallowed the hot coffee without tasting it. He asked one of the customers for directions to the Kings Highway station and was told it was about another dozen blocks.

He walked on, not paying much attention to what was around him, simply making sure he was following the directions that had been given to him. At the end of one block he had to wait for a car to pass before crossing the street. While he waited he saw that across from him on the other side was a synagogue. It was not an elaborate building. It had probably once been a private home. It looked old, shabby, the shrubbery and grass at its front, sparse.

He crossed the street and noted the name on a bronze plaque by the door, Congregation Shaare Tefilla. He'd only been in synagogues for friend's bar-mitzvahs, weddings, or funerals. He and Miriam had given their son Richard the option to have a bar-mitzvah. He'd chosen not to. Now for some reason he couldn't explain, Alex pulled the door open and went inside.

He found himself in a foyer with closed doors on either side. There were no ornaments or decorations, just a bulletin board on one wall, with various announcements on it. It was quiet. It felt as if he was the only one in the building. He looked at the doors to see if there were signs on them indicating what might be behind them, but there were none.

Then the door through which he had come opened. He turned around and saw a small man, a very small man, perhaps no more than four feet tall. His skin had a greenish pallor, his eyes bulged, making Alex think of a frog. He wore a tan suit that looked as if it had been slept in, no tie, and had a skull cap on his head.

"So? Who are you?" the frog asked, the voice a surprisingly deep, melodious baritone. "I go out for one minute and in comes a burglar?"

Alex held up his attaché case. "Do I look like a burglar?"

"Who knows what a burglar looks like? You should be wearing a black stocking over your head? For all I know you could be a serial killer and I'm the bowl of oatmeal."

Alex smiled. "What is this, the Comedy Club?"

"State your business. Are you a lawyer, come to sue me? Maybe you have briefs in that briefcase?" He pushed open the door nearest to him and Alex followed him into a room not much larger than a closet, fitted out with a desk and filing cabinet. He sat behind his desk. "Have a seat."

Alex sat, the case on his lap. "I'm not a lawyer. And I have no briefs. I saw this was a synagogue—"

"Keen powers of observation."

"I was curious—"

"Curiosity killed the cat."

Alex continued. "I was curious to see what it looked like."

"*Du bist a yid?*"

Alex did not speak Yiddish, but he knew the meaning of the ancient question: "Are you a Jew?" Most Jews had heard it at one time or another, usually when someone was in an unfamiliar place and looking for friendly contact. "Does it make any difference?"

Seated behind the desk the dwarf was less intimidating. Apparently his diminished size was caused by his legs because the upper part of his body looked normal. Additionally, he looked somewhat less like a frog although his face had serious pock-marks. "Of course you're a Jew." He shrugged. "I was only asking to make polite conversation. What is it you are curious about?"

The deep baritone voice was also no longer incongru-
ous. Its musicality reminded Alex of one of the actors in a
Shakespearean movie he had seen a long time ago. He
could not quite remember which actor or which movie. "I
wanted to see what the Temple looked like."

"You mean you don't remember?"

"I remember. But I haven't been in one in a long time."

"And why is that?" He did not wait for an answer.
"Don't tell me. I know. You lost your faith."

"I never had it to lose."

"Another Jewish atheist. Dear God, there are so many
of you." He patted the yarmulke on the top of his head. "I
wonder sometimes if we're going to survive. Who needed
the Holocaust? The best way to wipe out the Jews is to
open up the world to them. Then what do they do? They
inter-marry and raise their children telling them they
should decide for themselves what they are going to be. A
mishegoss, that what it is. A conundrum. A helluva way to
run a railroad."

"I wasn't given a choice. My father taught me to be an
atheist."

"He should be ashamed of himself."

"He's dead."

"Then he can't influence you anymore. Think about it.
Maybe, perhaps, he was wrong."

"He was wrong about a lot of things."

With difficulty, the man got off the chair and came
around the side of the desk. "You want to see the shul?
Come on, I'll show you."

Alex followed him to the door at the far end of the corridor. Behind that door was a flight of stairs.

"The sanctuary is upstairs." They went up. "By the
way, in case you haven't guessed, I'm the *shammes,* the
sexton. There isn't anything I don't know about this shul.
I was here from the beginning."

"I assume it was a private house."

"You assume correctly. Which is why we had to make the upstairs for the sanctuary. The way the house was built, the largest space was on the second floor."

At the head of the stairs was a landing enclosed by a wrought-iron gate. "For safety. We didn't want anyone dizzy from the exaltation of communing with God falling down a flight of stairs, God forbid. And suing us, besides."

The stairs had led them to what was the back of the Temple. Alex had expected little and was surprised by what he saw. His first impression was of form and symmetry giving the room a serene presence. The walls were paneled in a pale oak with rows of benches, also made of light oak. Each bench seated four; there were two to a row divided by an aisle. There was a pulpit at the far end and behind it a cabinet made of the same pale wood, the front of which had doors inlaid with mother-of-pearl and further adorned with intricate carvings. From where he stood he could not discern the details of the carvings, but he was struck by the shafts of light that poured down on them from an enormous skylight in the roof. The brightness filled the room and gave it a mystical glow.

"There was a third floor to the house, which we took out in order to get the height. I call it a *yiddishe* ceiling. After all, it's not a cathedral. Beautiful isn't it?"

"Very beautiful."

"It's a small congregation, but faithful." They stood there a few moments in silence, then the sexton said, "Okay? Seen what you came for?"

"Could you do me a favor? Could I stay here a few minutes?

The sexton once again shrugged. "I'll be in my office. Just let me know when you're done." He started down the stairs.

"You're not afraid to leave me here alone?"

The man turned and for the first time smiled, revealing a row of beautiful white teeth. "*Bubbele*, the only damage I think you might do up here is to yourself." He continued down the stairs.

Alex walked down the aisle and stopped about halfway to the front. He moved sideways along one of the benches as if he were maneuvering past someone's legs, then sat down in the middle. In front of him was a receptacle with two books with blue covers. He took one and read its title in gold capitals: "The New Union Prayer Book", and in smaller type, "Weekdays, Sabbaths, and Festivals." On the front cover was another title, "Gates Of Prayer, and on the back cover were Hebrew letters which he guessed translated into "Gates of Prayer." He opened the book and discovered that what he thought was the front was actually the back. Although there seemed to be as much English as Hebrew the pages ran from right to left. He turned pages, not reading anything but odd sentences out of context:

We are encompassed by questions to which we can only respond with awe.

Which is the right path to choose? One that is honorable in itself and also wins honor from others.

Was I honorable with Rudi and Francesca?

If I am not for myself, who will be for me? But if I am only for myself, what am I?

He looked up once again at the skylight. How strange it felt to be here in this beautiful and holy place.

He read more:

Give meaning to my life and substance to my hopes; help me understand those about me and fill me with the desire to serve them. Let me not forget that I depend on others as they depend on me...

Miriam. Does she need me now? Does prayer help?

People come here to pray. He had never prayed, so he had no idea what you could get from it.

෧෨෧෨

There had not been a service for his father. But the night before they had all gone to sit beside the coffin. His mother was dry-eyed. After a while, Alex went into the hall and lit his pipe. His hand shook enough to cause ashes to spill out of the pipe. He walked to the end of the corridor where a window looked out onto a lot filled with tires, a refrigerator with the door missing, black garbage bags, scraps of newspaper fluttering like flags.

He turned and saw his son Richard approaching. He walked with the ease and grace of a dancer.

Richard took a pack of cigarettes out of his pocket.

"I didn't know you smoked," Alex said.

"There's lots of things you don't know about me."

"Why don't you tell me some?"

"You don't really want to know."

"I do. Talk to me."

Richard blew smoke at the ceiling. "It doesn't seem very appropriate now. Maybe some other time."

Alex reached out and touched his son's face. He remembered Richard as an infant lying in his arms. "Yes. Maybe some other time."

෧෨෧෨

He turned pages again, going forward and backward until one paragraph stopped him. And he read:

If God is not, then the existence of all that is beautiful and…good, is but the accidental…by-product of blindly swirling atoms…Atheism leads…only to an incurable sadness and loneliness.

He took a long deep breath. How could there be a God? How do you explain war and torture and genocide and mass rape and the killing of babies? The Holocaust? Where was God when the roof blew off a church in Alabama, killing the parishioners who were in the middle of praying to Him? Where was he when his father did what he did when Clarice decided to commit suicide? Could it be that old son of a bitch Devil is more powerful than that old son of a bitch Jehovah?

Back in college, he had had a crush on a girl who was a devout Catholic. He had presented his argument: People all over the world believed. Did it make their lives better? In the name of their God they killed. In their God's name, they were killed. The holy books that were read for centuries contained the holy words for the believers to follow. But there were as many interpretations of those words as there were intermediaries to interpret them.

Her answer was simple. The Pope was God's deputy. Whatever he said, she believed. "Faith," she said. "I have faith. With that faith, I don't need anything else."

To his delighted surprise she went to bed with him, atheist Jew that he was. "The Pope doesn't have to know everything," she explained.

He thought he might have fallen asleep. He looked around. He was still alone. He stood up, sidled out into the aisle, and went back downstairs.

The door to the sexton's office was open. He was seated at his desk, leaning back in his chair. "*Nu?*"

"Thank you very much."

"And are you now converted?"

"Not quite. But maybe I'm on the way."

The sexton waved a hand. "Maybe, perhaps."

Alex raised his in reply and went out into the street.

Unwillingly he saw Francesca's face, the tears running, heard her cry. He did not want to hurt anyone. Why couldn't they see that? All he wanted was the right, the right he shouldn't be denied, to know his own flesh and blood.

Chapter 26

He got on the train at Kings Highway and not long after, closed his eyes. When there was a stop he listened to the opening and closing of the doors and heard the movement of the passengers. His mind kept returning to the synagogue, to the sanctuary, the light streaming in, the mystical feel of the place. He'd felt at peace there, the real world far away.

Occasionally, he opened his eyes, sometimes meeting the stare of the person seated opposite, an unblinking stare that seemed to be judging him, demanding something of him that he wasn't prepared to give.

He didn't get off at the Prince Street stop near his office. There was no way he could go back to work. If Roth didn't like it, tough shit. Instead, he went on to 34th Street for Penn Station and the Long Island Railroad. From there he could get a train home. The underground corridors were full of determined people, all in a big hurry. He felt no connection to them. He felt more like one of the creatures from the movie they'd seen, *Close Encounters of the Third Kind.* Everyone around him seemed to be objects, rather than humans, all part of a strange landscape. He decided he didn't want to go home either. Miriam was there with her own problems. She didn't need him and she didn't want him. The way he felt now he couldn't do her any good. When he looked up and saw the exit sign for 34th Street, he took it.

He found himself in front of Madison Square Garden. As always, in that neighborhood, there was movement, color, and sound. Throngs hurried along the sidewalk in front of him passing each other briskly in their determined journeys, nobody making eye contact but managing to avoid crashing into each other by the use of inner-city radar. Taxis swarmed, horns blasted as pedestrians jumped in front of them and then out of their way while the lights changed from red to green to red again. Street people shoved flyers into his face. He put up his free hand and pushed through them as if they were cobwebs.

He turned off Seventh Avenue onto one of the numbered streets. He didn't know or care which one it was. He stopped in front of a bar, the kind of old-fashioned neighborhood place that looked as if it had been there forever, the kind of bar he'd gone to once as a teenager, on St. Patrick's Day, on a dare. It was in the Rockaways, an area called "Irishtown." He'd heard that wild drinking and partying went on. He'd gone there with his friend, Robby Gold, to see what it was like. They'd been a bit disappointed because all they saw were guys waving beer bottles around, although there was a certain amount of excitement when they wondered if they'd get beaten up if the Irishers found out they were Jews.

The Old English lettering on the plate glass window spelled out, *Delaney's Bar & Grill.* He went in and found it wasn't dark and dreary, as he'd expected and neither the customers nor the bartender looked at him as if he were an invader of their space.

The bartender was a woman, in her twenties he guessed, with loose blonde hair and a quick smile. She wore a tight tee shirt with writing on it that he could not make out because she was in constant motion, wiping glasses, moving bottles, cleaning, getting ice. There were only three other customers, two men seated next to each other and a woman at the other end of the bar. He chose a stool between them. He put his attaché case on the floor and ordered a Dewar's on the rocks, laying a $20 dollar bill on the counter. She poured his drink, took his money, returned with his change, and went back to doing her thing.

Alex sipped his Dewar's, then reached into his pocket for his pipe and tobacco pouch. He held up the pipe for the bartender to see. "Okay if I smoke this in here?"

"Hey, guy, smoke whatever you want, long as it ain't dope."

One of the men sitting at his left said, "What's the matter with dope? If you use it right, it's fine."

"That's right," the woman a few stools away on the other side of Alex said. "As a matter of fact, it's therapeutic. They give it to people who have cancer." She looked at Alex and smiled.

The bartender said, "I'm not arguing with you. I didn't say I'm for it or against it. I just said, not in here. We don't want any blue-jackets making unannounced visits."

Alex filled the bowl and lit it. He took a few puffs and watched the smoke drift in front of him.

The woman said, "I always loved the smell of pipe tobacco. It's a kid thing, I guess. I used to have a crush on this senior in high school. He smoked a pipe. He kept it in his mouth all the time. Not in school, I mean where he hung out in front of the school. He used to stand with his jaw stuck out and the pipe jutting out of it. He looked like John Wayne. And I'd walk past and smell his tobacco and think he was the greatest thing on two legs. He never noticed me, though."

"Too bad," Alex said.

"You have the same kind of jaw. Big. Strong. And I like that little scar at the side of your mouth."

"I fell off a bike when I was a kid."

"What are you doing here?"

"I beg your pardon?" Alex now looked more closely at her and what he saw was exotic, or an attempt to be—straight black hair with bangs, olive skin, a wide red mouth, long shimmering earrings. She wore a tight, black top over a short black skirt. She had to be Hispanic or Greek or Israeli, not as young as the bartender, but not much older.

"A strange question?" She smiled. "Well, I know you're not a regular. I've never seen you before. Also, you've got a look about you, like you're distracted like you don't really know what you're doing."

Her voice did not match her looks. It was high-pitched and a bit muted. He would have expected something more musical. "Well, at least I know what you do for a living," Alex said.

"You do?"

"Sure. You're a Gypsy fortune teller. You read the past and the future out of the bottom of bar glasses."

She held up a hand, long fingernails painted silver. "I'm sorry. That was very insensitive of me. I didn't mean to poke into your privacy."

"That's okay. I'm a little jumpy. I didn't mean to be so sarcastic, either. Just a lot of things going on. You know how it is."

"Oh yes. I think everyone knows how it is." She raised her glass, which was filled with some kind of orange-colored liquid, and drained it down. "Toni."

The blonde bartender took her empty glass away and came back with a full one. "Take it out of mine," Alex said. And I'll have another, too. When he had his fresh drink, he raised the glass in the direction of the woman. "Cheers."

"Thanks," she said, raising her glass, "*A vos amours.*"

"Why don't we just stick to Cheers? Love is too complicated."

Her smile seemed genuine. "Okay, Cheers."

One of the other customers put coins into a jukebox and a song began playing that Alex didn't recognize. His companion swayed and hummed. "I love this kid Michael Jackson. I love the music, the energy."

"Yeah. Sounds pretty good."

"You want to dance?"

"No. I don't think so."

"You're shy."

"That's right."

"I'm a great dancer. I could teach you."

"Thanks, but no thanks." He emptied his glass and held it up again, for the bartender to refill. He put another bill on the counter.

"You don't want to go too fast with those," his neighbor said. "They have a way of sneaking up on you."

He took a deep breath. "Look, Miss…" He didn't know her name.

"Honey. Honey Bunch." Then quickly added, "That's my stage name. I'm an actress."

"Miss…Bunch…I think, if you take a good look at me, you will see that I have long since passed the age where I need someone to advise me when or how or why I should or should not have a drink."

"Hey! *Excusez-moi.* I'm not trying to interfere with your life. I was just being neighborly." She turned away from him.

He sipped more Scotch. It was beginning to have no taste. A new song was now playing. This one sounded more familiar. He tried to listen to it to see if he actually might know some music that wasn't a hundred years old, but in spite of his concentration, he could not place it.

"I'm sorry," he heard whispered into his ear.

She had moved. She was now on the stool next to his. Her drink was side by side with his on the bar along with her pocketbook, a large one made of what looked like a tapestry. "I'm sorry," she repeated. "I was out of line. Certainly it's not my business what you drink or how much you drink. We all have our own scores to settle."

He didn't say anything.

She nudged him. "Okay? Am I forgiven? We're friends again?"

"Sure."

"So what's your name? Since we're friends I ought to know your name."

"JimBob," he said, surprising himself, and put on what he hoped was a southwestern accent. "JimBob McCafferty at your service."

"That's a southern name, right?"

"Right as rain. Right outta the glorious state of Texas." He heard himself drawl the words. He watched as she shook her head and light gleamed in her sleek black hair. "I grew up on a five-thousand-acre ranch. It was named Faith, Hope, and Charity after my three aunts who my grandfather loved more than anything in the world, except for my grandmother who they say was the prettiest thang in the whole state." He smiled, trying to remember where he had read a story like that once, and also at how easily the hokum came out of his mouth.

"I never would've guessed," she said.

"Is that right?"

"Never. I figured you for a native New Yorker."

"I hear tell there ain't no such thing as a native New Yorker. That everyone comes from someplace else."

"That's right," she said. "You see them on TV all the time when they do those stupid interviews. `I come from Keeokuk, Iowa. I've been in New York two months and it's like home to me now.' And there's always a famous model who's so gorgeous you could plotz from the way she looks, and she speaks in this voice like liquid Sweet n' Low, 'N'Orlins, that's wheah om from, but I luvvv, New Yolk.' Me? I'm from Queens and everyone I know is from Brooklyn."

He laughed. "Miss Bunch, I see your glass is empty. Let me buy you another of whatever that strange thing is you're drinking."

"It's a Harvey Wallbanger. I love them. And call me Honey, okay? We're friends now, right?" She called out, "Toni."

The blonde bartender came over to where they were and put both hands flat on the bar. He could see the writing on her shirt clearly now. It read, "Life Sucks and Then You Die."

"I hope you don't believe that," he said.

"What?"

"What you're wearing."

"You don't like it?"

"It's awfully pessimistic."

"But true. That's what it all boils down to."

"Come on now," Honey said. "What's with all this gloom and doom? I want you to meet my friend here. Jim-Bob. From Texas."

"Charmed," the bartender said, "I'm sure."

"JimBob wants to buy me another drink."

"And you, too," Alex said.

"Thanks. I don't drink."

Alex nodded in approval. "Very wise." He swirled the ice in his glass. "I think I will have just one more. Then I've got to go."

"So soon? We're just getting to know each other." Honey let one hand rest on his thigh.

The touch of her hand startled him. He felt the heat of her palm through the fabric of his trousers. The bartender returned with their drinks. He lifted his glass and swallowed some of the liquid. He could not detect the taste of the Scotch at all now and was vaguely aware that it might be a signal that maybe he had already had too much to drink.

"So whaddya think, JimBob?" Honey's hand still rested on his thigh. With the other she sipped from her glass.

He looked at her mouth, which had lost some of its lipstick but was warm and inviting, the lips parted slightly, a glint of white teeth, a cave, a burrow to explore, a place to find comfort and unknown secrets. "About what?"

She whispered into his ear. "Do you want to come home with me?"

He took another swallow and then he was back in the synagogue, light flooding in from the skylight onto the book open in front of him. He could see the words on the page, they were wavering but he could make them out: "...*We are encompassed by questions...Which is the right path to choose?...If I am not for myself, who will be for me?...*"

"Did I tell you about my son?" he said.

"You have a son? That's really nice."

"He's a good kid. Got problems."

"Who doesn't? I mean, who doesn't?"

"He wants to be an actor."

"Tell him to get in line."

"That's not all. It's more serious than that. I think he's gay."

"You call that a problem? If that's a problem, half the world's got a problem." She squeezed his thigh.

His head seemed to clear a little. He leaned over to her. "Are you...professional?"

"Of course not. But I have to live, you know? Surviving in this town is an art form."

"I haven't got much money."

"Don't worry about it. We'll play it by ear." She drained her glass and picked up her oversize purse. "Let's go, JimBob. Let's head out yonder and see what's out there on the range."

He swallowed what was left in his glass, at the same time took an ice cube between his teeth and crushed it, savoring the bits of ice melting in his mouth. He left what remained of his change for a tip and retrieved his briefcase from the floor. "So long, Toni," he said.

"See ya," Honey Bunch said.

They walked west toward the Hudson. The sun had set and the streets were darkening with shadows. Neither spoke. Nor did they touch. They crossed Ninth Avenue and went a quarter of the way up the block where she turned into one of a row of similar buildings. It had four steps leading to a small entrance. Inside, he slowly followed her up a staircase that seemed endless.

"I'm on the top floor." She was breathing hard. "Great aerobics just to get up here."

He was having trouble breathing himself. He knew he shouldn't be doing this, but he gave himself the excuse that he'd had too much to drink.

She opened the door and he followed her inside. "Excuse the mess. I didn't have a chance to tidy up."

There wasn't any floor you could see. Every scrap of available space was taken up by pillows, newspapers, magazines, dishes, cups, glasses, ashtrays. There were jackets, blouses, pants, skirts, all kinds of shoes. The wreckage extended to a chair, a couch, a coffee table, and in one corner, a bed.

"What mess?" he mumbled.

He moved forward and stepped on a boot, which made him lose his balance. He let go of the attaché case and threw his arms out to keep from falling. He managed to stay upright, but an extreme dizziness got hold of him. The room began to move haphazardly. He hoped he wouldn't throw up.

"Are you okay?" Honey took his arm. "Come over here. Sit down. Take a load off." She led him to the couch and made room for him by pushing everything onto the floor. "I'm not much of a housekeeper."

"Couldda fooled me."

He let himself sink into the softness of the couch. His mind briefly cleared. *Oh God*, he thought. *What am I doing here? How did I let myself get into this?* His head became fuzzy again and the nausea returned. His eyes were closing.

The dwarf from the synagogue was tugging at his arm. He woke up to see Honey Bunch shaking him. "Time to wake up, Sleepy Head. We can't have you spending all night here."

"I guess I fell asleep."

"You went out like a light. I let you have ten minutes, but I got things to do too, you know."

"I guess I had too much to drink."

"You might say that. Want to use the john?"

"Good idea." He pushed himself up and maneuvered into the bathroom. The walls were purple, the light a bare bulb hanging from a wire surrounded by a Japanese paper globe. He used the toilet, splashed some cold water on his face, and washed his hands. He was still feeling dizzy and nauseous. When he came out Honey held out a glass. "What's this?"

"Cold ginger ale. Drink it. It's good for you."

Thirsty, he gulped it down. It was good.

She took the glass from him and placed it on a table cluttered with ashtrays. He sat on the couch and put his head back, his eyes closing again. He heard her moving about. She was humming a tune he had never heard before. After a while, he heard her approach and felt her leg next to his. The musky odor of her perfume slid up his nostrils. Then her hand was on his pants and over his fly.

"Whaddya say, JimBob." Honey's scratchy whisper in his ear. "Feeling a little better?"

"A little."

"So whaddya say?" He could feel her getting at the zipper of his fly.

He opened his eyes and tried to sit up. "Wait a minute."

"What's the matter?"

"I don't think I want to do this."

She didn't remove her hand but stopped trying to get at the zipper. "What do you mean?"

"I mean...I think I changed my mind. I don't think I want to do it anymore."

Honey peered at him. "You shittin me? I thought you were all hot to trot." Her long earrings glittered as light from a lamp in the corner reflected off them. "What happened, JimBob, lost your nerve?"

He struggled again to sit up. He had to get out of this. He'd only been with a prostitute once in his life. The year Clarice died he'd quit school and was working out west on a ranch. The other ranch hands dragged him to a bar. The hooker they bought him was old and experienced. She had rolls of fat on her belly and smelled of sour beer.

But that wasn't the real reason. It was because he felt dirty, ashamed that he'd allowed himself to sink this low. "I had too much to drink," he said, hoping she'd accept that explanation. "I don't really feel good."

Her eyes became dull, and her voice was like Brando in *The Godfather*. "Let me explain something. We had a deal. I didn't bring you up here for nothing, you know."

He noticed a poster on the wall in front of him. It showed the bare behind of a man bending over and pulling his cheeks apart. In the place where his asshole should have been was a grinning mouth.

Honey was smiling again. With one hand she pushed back against his chest, with the other she was again at his zipper. "Trust me. Honey Bunch delivers what she promises."

"No." He pushed her away from him and got to his feet. "No. I mean it. I don't want you to do anything. But don't worry, I'll pay you."

"Well, that's different," Honey said. "In that case, whatever you want is okay with me."

"How much do I owe you?"

"How about fifty?"

He pulled three twenty-dollar bills out of his wallet. She took it from him with the tips of her fingers as if she were accepting a flower. "A ten-dollar tip? How nice."

She reached down, picked up his briefcase, and handed it to him. Then she took his arm and moved him toward the door. "Ready to go?"

He nodded and reached for the doorknob.

"JimBob." Her long silver nails gleamed in the dim light. "Wait."

He stopped.

"Before you go, I want to tell you something."

He could not be sure, because she was not smiling, but he thought he could detect a glimmer of laughter in her eyes.

"What?"

"You know what, JimBob, or whatever your real name is? You're no more from Texas than I'm from the moon. But this is real." She took his free hand and guided it in a sudden movement to her crotch. Through the thin material of the skirt, he felt a familiar mass. He tried to pull his hand away but she held it firmly against her so there was no mistaking what it was he was feeling.

"Jesus," he said. "Jesus H. Christ."

Now she was grinning, white teeth showing. Her face

was like a glow of neon, bright colors pulsing in front of his eyes. She opened the door and pushed him gently but firmly into the hall. "Have a nice day."

The door closed behind him. He stood there, arms at his side, bewildered. He heard a loud click. Honey Bunch had locked the door.

Chapter 27

Miriam was glad Alex had gone to work. She needed to be alone. She had a lot to think about. But first, she had to deal with the pain. The incision they'd made in her breast hurt as if a fragment of glass had lodged there. She'd left the hospital full of painkillers but they were no longer working. The nurse had given her a couple of hydrocodone pills to take home and a prescription for more if needed. She swallowed them now with a glass of water. The problem would be solved, at least temporarily. If it got worse, she'd have to get the prescription filled.

Physical pain was one thing. What was going on in her mind was the real problem. The specter of cancer had come as a tremendous shock. It brought up all kinds of questions, none of which she had an answer to. Who was she, this Miriam Gunther? A forty-one-year-old woman, married with one child. What was she going to do with her life, at least with what she had left of it? Was she going to try to keep her marriage? Or was it already too late? What had she done thus far with her life? Not much.

She was too tense to stay in one place. She wandered through the house, going to all the floors, from the basement to the attic. Old suitcases in there, discarded furniture, unused picture frames she remembered buying a long time ago when she and Alex went antiquing in

Connecticut. She went downstairs to the dining room. They'd had lots of good times here. Birthday parties, dinner parties, Thanksgiving. Maybe she should invite friends over for dinner? It might help to do that. The same moment she thought it, she knew she wouldn't do it.

Upstairs, she paused at the door of Richard's bedroom. She couldn't believe it was almost a year since he'd left, taking one meager suitcase, and insisting he go to the train station alone.

"I'll be fine," he told them. "Don't worry."

Eighteen and wanting to go out on his own. And for what? To be an actor!

She went inside and sat on his bed. They shouldn't have been surprised. He'd gotten involved with the theater group in his first year in high school. He helped build sets, and learned all about theater. In his second year, he began to perform.

"It's the only time I enjoy being in school," he'd told them. "The teachers don't like me. I get picked on. If it weren't for that, I'd drop out."

The truth was that he was a mediocre student. His grades were just above passing. And he hated studying.

Nevertheless, they'd argued and argued trying to persuade him to go to college.

"They have theater groups in college."

Richard shook his head. He had light brown curly hair that he'd let grow long. Where had the curls come from? She and Alex both had straight hair. But he had his father's sea-blue eyes and those long eyelashes. "You don't understand. I want to be an actor. What good would college do me?"

She'd sympathized with him because she'd had almost the same argument with her mother when she was that age. She hadn't gone to college either.

Surprisingly, Alex gave in first. "If that's what you

want, we'll help you as much as we can. With one caveat. If you don't get anywhere in a year, you'll go to college."

Richard happily agreed.

The room was neat now, unlike the mess it had always been—bedding unmade, socks, underwear, shoes, books scattered all over. Three posters were still on the wall above his bed. David Bowie, Pink Floyd, Marlon Brando.

She remembered how many times she tried to get him to straighten up his room. "Later, Mom. I promise." She'd given up and handled it by keeping the door to his room closed.

He wasn't an easy child. When he was about five he'd become difficult about food. He wouldn't eat hot cereal. For cold cereal he only wanted the sugared kind. Frosted Flakes, the worst. But she'd gone along. It was easier than having a battle every day.

About that same time, he began to wear her jewelry and clomp around in her high heels. Alex had been very upset about it. "He's a boy. He shouldn't be dressing up in girls' clothes."

"I think he looks adorable. He's having fun, that's all. Besides, how can I get him to stop? Threaten him? What good would it do?"

She still wasn't sure if Richard was gay. He'd never said anything, nor would they ever ask. As far as she knew, he'd never had a lover of either sex. Perhaps he was still finding his sexuality.

She'd always given in to him. And why not? She didn't care about anything but his happiness. Now he was in a play they were going to see at the end of the week. That was promising, wasn't it?

She went back to the kitchen to make a cup of tea. She filled the kettle with water and set it on the stove. She took a bag from the box of Lipton tea in the cupboard and dropped it into a mug. When the kettle began to shriek she poured the boiling water into the mug and took it to the table. She added one spoonful of sugar. The ritual calmed her. She held the mug in both hands, enjoying the warmth. *Face it, she told herself. You may be dead soon. Breast cancer can strike fast.* She'd heard that one of her high school friends had recently died of it. Of course, she would have to wait for the results of the biopsy. But if what she suspected was true, what should she do? What could she do? She blew on the tea and took a sip. The house was very quiet. The only sound was the humming of the refrigerator.

When she'd had enough of the tea, she went to the phone and called her mother.

"How are you, darling? How are you feeling?" Her mother's voice was like gravel rolled in honey.

"Not too bad. I just wanted to say hello and thank you for being there for me yesterday."

"What? You're thanking me for being a mother?"

"No. For being a wonderful mother. And it was nice of Henry to be there."

"That's a good one. You think he wanted to come? No way. I made him."

"Why would you do that?"

"It's good for men to be told what to do."

"Is that what you did with Dad?"

Mabel laughed. "I didn't have to. He was the sweetest man that ever lived. One in a million."

"I'll bet you still miss him after all these years."

"Of course I do. I still dream about him. Funny, isn't it?"

"I think you were a very lucky woman."

"I know I was. But let's get back to square one. What are you doing with yourself? Do you have any pain?"

"Just a little. Nothing to worry about."

"Would you like me to come over? Is there anything I can do for you?"

"You already did it, Mom. Just talking to you has made me feel much better."

When she hung up she thought of her father. He was only forty-eight when he had a heart attack and died. She was nine. Her memories had dimmed with the passing years but she still remembered holding his hand when they went on one of their Sunday excursions. He was an accountant for a large firm in the city and worked long hours, sometimes six days a week. But Sunday was their day. They would go out while her mother prepared a big dinner, usually roast beef with baked potatoes and creamed spinach. If the weather was nice they would often go to Prospect Park and the zoo. Sometimes they'd take a boat and row on the lake. Other days they went to the Botanical Gardens. In cold weather, they went to the Brooklyn Museum, or the library, where they had exhibits. Sometimes they took the subway into the city. The Museum of Natural History was her favorite place. There was so much to see. She especially loved the bird's eggs and the butterflies. Sometimes her father challenged her to remember the names, a challenge she relished because she knew most of them. She could still remember a few: *Monarch, Swallowtail, Zebra Longwing, Karner blue*. Afterward, they would buy roasted chestnuts from a vendor on the street.

Miriam's eyes filled. She patted them with a tissue and berated herself for becoming sentimental. *Let's get practical and stop drifting off into reminiscences*. She wished she'd done more with her life. She'd been a good student, got better than average grades but for some reason had no desire to study further, no particular desire to do anything.

She thought she ought to do something practical at least. Her idea was to enroll in a secretarial school to learn stenography and typing. One of her teachers had said those were great tools for women. It meant they could always get a job. And indeed, it did. It led to her working for Larry

Mitler. The work was fairly interesting but not satisfying. She wanted more, even though she had no idea what that was.

When she became aware that Larry was becoming interested in her, she wasn't sure how to handle it. It was also just about that time she began seeing Alex. She knew Mitler was married. He wasn't overly aggressive, no rubbing up against her or touching. If that had happened she would have told him off and walked out. But she had the feeling he was on the make all the time.

One night when they had worked later than usual, he'd said, "How would you feel about having dinner? You worked overtime so I owe you something."

She wanted him to know that was not going to happen. "Sorry, I'm meeting some friends, but thanks, anyway."

He didn't give up easily. Every once in a while he'd ask about dinner, but never pushed it when she refused. And she had to admit he had a certain charm about him. She was still working for him when she married Alex. He gave them a generous wedding gift.

A year or so later, she finally agreed to have lunch with him. That turned out to be a bad decision. Unfortunately, that was the day Alex had been in the neighborhood and came to the store looking for her. Someone in the shop told him they'd gone out to lunch and guessed where they might be. He came to the restaurant and saw them just as Mitler had put his hand on hers. When she looked up and saw Alex she pulled her hand away as if someone had put a lit cigarette on it. She prayed that Alex hadn't noticed.

A few months later she was pregnant. Alex had called and said he had to go out to dinner with a buyer. It was after midnight when he got home and she was asleep. The next thing she knew he woke her.

"He was here, wasn't he?"

"What…who…?"

"That cocksucker, Mitler. He was here, wasn't he? In this bed." He had his hands on her shoulders. He was shaking her.

She pushed herself up, awake now. "What are you talking about?"

"I can smell it. You were fucking. I can smell it." He let go of her and stood up.

"I was home alone the whole night. Nobody was here."

"You're having an affair with him. I knew it but I didn't say anything. I don't know why I didn't say anything, maybe I was too scared to find out. But now I want to know." He put his hand down hard on her belly. "Whose baby is this? Mine or his?"

"Don't be ridiculous." She got out of bed, her nightgown falling to just below her knees. "It's yours."

"Bullshit."

"I never had an affair with anyone."

He pushed her and she fell back hard on the bed. Her eyes opened wide, her mouth opened but no sound came out.

Then he was holding her against him, pressing his forehead against her swollen belly. "I'm sorry, I'm sorry. I didn't mean it."

"Alex, the baby is ours. Yours and mine."

Now he was sobbing. "I'm sorry. I'm sorry. I believe you. I didn't hurt you, did I?"

"You knocked the breath out of me a little, that's all."

"I'm a jackass. I know you would never do anything like that...would you?"

"No, never."

The pain was coming back. There was no alternative. She drove to the shopping center where the pharmacy was and handed in the prescription. The girl at the counter wore large hoop earrings and had green nails. She was told there would be a twenty-minute wait. Miriam strolled through the aisles. She bought some makeup and pondered the range of lipstick colors. Bright red was making a comeback *Vogue* had declared. Not for her. She chose a Revlon shade called *In the Red* but was actually quite light. The store was filled with customers. She had an urge to scream at them. *You all look so normal. But I'm not. I might be dying!*

She got the prescription and hurried out of the store.

Back home she took more pills and lay down on the couch in the den to wait for them to work. Even though the thermostat was set to 70 degrees she felt cold. She got a small down comforter from the closet and covered herself. In a little while she felt snug and warm. She'd noticed one of Alex's pipes on a table with a tin of tobacco beside it. She remembered when they first met how she'd enjoyed the aroma of his tobacco. She married Alex when she was nineteen. She thought she was so smart, thought she knew everything. When she first saw him in the Strand Bookstore and their eyes locked, she knew he was the one. Those beautiful blue eyes and those long dark lashes. "What a waste," she'd said to him. "Those eyes belong on a girl."

"Is that a compliment?" he'd said, smiling.

The early years had been everything she'd hoped for. They loved each other, liked, and admired each other. Their sex life was amazing. When Richard was born, it just made everything better. So what happened? Two decades later, it all seemed to have vanished. Did it happen slowly, and she hadn't noticed? She didn't have a specific time frame, but it had become obvious to her that Alex was becoming more and more distant. Or maybe she herself was the one putting distance between them?

She'd tried a few times to have a conversation with him about it. "No idea what you're talking about," had been his response. Then came the discovery of his father's diary.

She understood he'd never gotten over Clarice's suicide, and that he blamed himself for not having prevented it. She'd tried a few times over the years to get him to see a psychiatrist, but he'd refused. "I don't need help. I'm okay." But she knew that wasn't true.

The diary had made everything worse. It seemed to have taken over his life. They hardly talked anymore. He'd always been a person who touched. When they walked, his hand found hers. If they sat in a theater, his arm went around her. No more.

When wandering through the house earlier, she'd avoided their bedroom. She didn't want to be reminded of the nights she'd been unable to sleep, staring at the ceiling, asking herself why he no longer touched her. He'd loved her breasts. When they made love, he never failed to lick her nipples. He would lick each one slowly, tenderly, sending cascades of pleasure throughout her body. "You have the most beautiful breasts," he'd whispered. "They fit perfectly into the palm of my hand." What would happen now if she had to lose one, or possibly both? Would they ever make love again?

The pills were making her drowsy. She realized that eventually there would have to be an accounting. A decision would have to be made. Now, of course, was not the time.

She closed her eyes and slept.

Chapter 28

Alex stood in a phone booth, his eyes closed, the receiver at his ear. He heard the ringing at the other end. No one was answering. He suddenly realized he'd called Wanda, not Miriam. He quickly hung up the phone. Why had he done that? He didn't even know what he'd say to her. It had been an agonizing trek from where he'd left Honey Bunch. It had taken all his concentration to lift one foot and move that leg forward, place it down carefully, then do the same with the other. He breathed in the stink of piss and God knows what else and shoved the door open for air.

It was already dark. What time was it, anyway? He looked at his watch, but there wasn't enough light to see. It had to be late. He should have been home by now. He'd gone into the booth to call Miriam. She might be wondering what had happened to him. She might even be worried. Or not. She had her own problems. But he'd called Wanda. Did he think she could provide the succor he needed? He shook his head, wondering. He had no idea how he going to explain this to Miriam. He knew he should call her but he couldn't do it. At least, not yet.

He stepped out of the booth and walked to the corner to read the street signs. Ninth Avenue and 33rd Street. Good. It helped knowing where he was. The darkness of the night, in spite of the streetlamps and light from the stores, added to his feeling of isolation. He felt the need for some kind of warmth to replace the bleakness and disgust he felt with himself.

If only he had a friend he could confide in, but there was nobody. It wasn't like high school when he hung out with a bunch of guys. They used to talk about everything, especially sex. But even then the really deep concerns were kept hidden.

Early in his marriage, he'd joined a bowling league. The guys had become friends but they were the usual drinking buddies. The talk was the usual stuff, always about women, sports, and money. All really personal feelings were always kept behind a wall. Just once, that invisible barrier was breached. It happened the time John Mazzone's daughter was in the hospital in a coma after being hit by a speeding car. After a month-long vigil at her bedside, his wife got him to go bowling. He came to the alley and rolled balls, drank beer, and laughed at the dumb jokes. Then suddenly he stood up, and like Job in bowling shoes, shook his fist at the ceiling. "You prick," he cried. "I trusted You. I went to church Sundays and wept for what they did to You to make You suffer, wept for Your bloody hands and feet. But You were supposed to be suffering for us…so we could have a better life. Ain't that it? Ain't that what we pray for? And this is how You pay me back? This is what You do to me?" Then he hung his head and stood where he was, the tears running down his face, his shoulders shaking.

Everyone was embarrassed. You would think the guy had pulled down his pants and crapped on the floor. Nobody knew what to do. Everyone stood there and looked at him and then at each other, some with bowling balls in their hands, some with beer bottles, immobilized by this outburst of feeling. The poor bastard had broken the rules and nobody knew how to handle it.

He wondered why that memory had come back to him. What did it mean? That God wouldn't help him? He'd known that all along.

He began to walk. After a couple of blocks, the tightness in his legs began to ease. The lights from a diner drew him. He went in and found the men's room. He looked in the mirror. His eyes were red-rimmed, his skin mottled. There was lipstick on his right cheek and on his ear. He didn't remember when Honey had gotten it on him but now he was glad to find hot water and soap, digging his fingers into his face to make sure he removed every trace of it. He hoped he didn't reek of alcohol or perfume. He patted himself dry with paper towels and turned away from the bloodshot eyes that looked back at him scornfully from the mirror, trying to ignore them, as well as the lines that grooved his cheeks into a definition of age.

Now he felt hungry. At the counter he ordered a bowl of *chicken rice* as the counterman called it. The soup was hot, and not bad. Not as good as Miriam's. He looked at his watch. It was almost eight o'clock. He had to get home.

He went into the street again. There was a dull ache in his head, and a pounding in his ears, but his movement was improving. He passed both wary and alert citizens of the new world. They looked as if they knew where they were going. There were others who were not paying attention to anything, some with a brown bag in hand, the neck of the bottle inside barely visible.

...Which is the right path to choose?...

He found his way to Penn Station, and bought a ticket. The next train would be thirty minutes. He sat in the waiting room feeling like shit. His temples throbbed, and his mouth was a sewer. He knew he should call Miriam, but he was too tired to get up. On the other hand, he could take the train to Long Beach and Wanda. Would she let him stay? Or was it all fantasy? Why was he even thinking of it?

His eyes closed and his mind drifted. When Clarice died nothing seemed to matter anymore. He quit school without telling anyone. He just packed a suitcase and took off.

Ames, Iowa. He knew nothing about it, heard the name somewhere. It was west. That was important. It seemed the only direction in which to go. He stayed there a while, then went on. He took buses from one town to the next. He was able to get odd jobs to keep him going. He took any kind of job he could get. He worked in supermarkets, gas stations, and laundromats. When he had saved enough money, he bought a bus ticket and moved on to the next town.

The first month he spoke to no one. His family did not know where he was. He knew they'd be worried, but he told himself he didn't care. Eventually, he called home to tell them he was safe.

"Come back," his mother said. "Go back to school. What good is this going to do?"

"Clarice is dead. And I know why."

"How is your running away going to help?"

"I'm not running away. I just don't want to be there anymore."

His father did not speak to him when he called but passed a message to him through his mother. "Tell him he's a damn fool. Anyone who'd rather be a bum than go to college is a damn fool."

In New Mexico, he got a job on a sheep ranch. He did everything from building fences to shearing sheep. He was up at five and asleep at seven. He no longer had nightmares. He ate every ounce of food that was put in front of him and lost weight. But his body grew hard, and for the first time, he began to think that maybe he would in the end go back.

He woke up in time to catch the train home. He wondered what he was going to say to Miriam.

Chapter 29

The walk from the station to his house cleared his head. He opened the side door that led into the kitchen, still not sure of anything except that he would not tell Miriam about Honey Bunch.

The entire house was dark but he didn't need to turn on a light because the street lamps provided enough illumination through the windows for him to see. He put his briefcase on the table and climbed the stairs to their bedroom. It was possible that Miriam was already asleep. He hoped not, because taking a shower in their bathroom might wake her. No matter. He desperately needed one.

There was no one in the bedroom. He stripped, threw everything in the laundry basket, except for his suit and tie. He bundled them up and put them on a shelf in his closet. They would go to the cleaners when he had a chance.

He made the water as hot as he could stand it, closed his eyes, and let the water rain down, hoping it would help remove the stench of the day. He brushed his teeth and rinsed his mouth with Listerine, got into pajamas, robe, and slippers, and went back downstairs to find Miriam.

She was in the den, lying on the sofa. He hesitated, not sure if he should wake her.

"I'm not asleep," she said. "I heard you come in."

"Oh? Why didn't you say anything?"

"Like what? Hello? Where have you been? I've got other things to think about. But it is late, isn't it?"

"Very. It's almost ten o'clock. You want to know why I'm so late?"

"Not really."

He switched on the table lamp next to the sofa. She was still dressed, wearing a gray blouse and black slacks. The light caused her to throw her hand across her eyes.

"Wow. That's bright. I've been lying in the dark too long."

"How are you feeling?"

"Like shit. Thanks for asking."

"What'd you do all day?"

"The truth?"

"Yeah."

"Moped. Sat around moping." She rubbed her eyes. "I did a lot of thinking, too. About life. About death. About our life together. Some of it was pretty good."

"A lot of it was pretty good."

"So where did it go off the rails?" She held up both hands. "Never mind. Don't bother to answer. I'd say we've been down that road too many times already." She got to her feet. "You hungry? I could make you something."

"No thanks. But I wouldn't mind a cup of coffee."

"I could use one, too."

He sat at the kitchen table while she made the coffee. When it was ready, she brought it to the table and sat across from him. The light in the kitchen was bright. He could see her eyes were streaked with red, dark smudges under them. She wore no makeup and her skin was pale. Pangs of guilt swept through him. "You look tired."

"Don't remind me what I look like. Something you might step on in the street."

He laughed. "Not that bad." He drank some coffee. "You really aren't interested in what I did today?"

"Sounds like you want to tell me, so go ahead."

In spite of his feelings of guilt, he now felt a sense of relief. He could tell her everything and just leave out the Honey part. Surprisingly, this intensified his guilt. Well, he'd been a shit and he deserved to suffer for it.

"You knew I wanted to see Rudy, my father's old friend. Well, I did it today. I went there and I found out I was right. He knew all along about my father's affair. He knew all about it."

"That's pretty interesting."

"There's more. He married the girl. He married the girl my father was fucking."

"No kidding," Miriam said.

"Then I blew it. I demanded to know where my sister was. They wouldn't tell me. I yelled. I wanted to throw things. Didn't matter. They absolutely refused to tell me anything."

"Why?"

"She was never told about it. They brought her up to believe he was her father. They said it would be too upsetting for her to find out now."

Miriam put her cup down. "I can see that. It's understandable."

"Sure, but where does that leave me?"

"In limbo, I'm afraid."

"But what happened after I left them is the main thing I want to tell you."

He told her about the temple, and about the dwarf. He told her about sitting in the sanctuary and how he read passages from the Bible. And how he had this kind of spiritual feeling. Not a revelation but something he couldn't explain to himself or to her. "I didn't know what it meant. Or if it meant anything. I only know that I felt different when I left there."

"What do you mean, different?"

"That's just it. I don't know. I wandered around. I went into the city. I didn't know what to do with myself. I went into a bar. I got drunk."

"Drunk? A nice Jewish boy like you, getting drunk in a bar? That doesn't sound like spirituality to me."

"The drunk part wasn't, but the feelings in the synagogue were."

"It seems to me that maybe life is catching up to you."

He sighed. "Is it ever."

"Speaking of life, I just want to remind you that this Saturday is the opening of Richard's play. We're all going. My mother and Henry will meet us there. We'll take Richard out afterward. Okay?"

"Oh yeah. *Iago's Dance of Death.* I wouldn't want to miss that for anything in the world."

Miriam glared at him. "You're doing it again. Making fun of him. Don't you realize you're demeaning your own son? When will you ever learn to be proud of him?"

"I'm not trying to demean him. But you're right. Sarcasm wasn't called for."

"That's really not good enough."

"Okay. I know I haven't been the greatest father in the world."

"You tried. But you didn't try hard enough. And I think you know why."

"What are you saying? Not that effeminate business again."

"Yes. That again. You won't admit it. But it was all because he wasn't what you expected. You thought a boy should be good at sports. He wasn't good. But did you give him credit for trying?" She put her cup down and he could see tears in her eyes. "He was out there with you for hours with baseballs, footballs. He just couldn't do it. So you gave up on him."

"You know it's not that simple."

"Then tell me I'm wrong. Tell me you weren't afraid he'd turn out to be gay."

"Jesus H. Christ." He pushed his chair back and stood up. "It's no use. I thought we were having a real conversation for a change. I thought we were getting somewhere, but we're back to where we were. I'm going to bed."

"Fine," Miriam said. "Keep doing what you've been doing lately. Run and hide."

Alex trudged up the stairs to the bedroom wondering how many times in one day he could fuck things up.

Chapter 30

The Festival Theater was on West 59th Street, close to Tenth Avenue. He shuddered, realizing it wasn't that far from Honey Bunch. He drove around several blocks searching for a space. He'd grown up in Brooklyn and now lived on Long Island, but in his mind, he would always be a New Yorker. And New Yorkers did not go to a garage until they had scoured the streets like a ravenous dog looking for food. When he finally spotted one, the feeling of triumph was palpable.

He and Miriam had barely spoken since the other night when they'd had the argument about their son. They were back to that uneasy truce they'd been living under for so many months.

She'd been right, of course, much as he refused to admit it. He'd been afraid that Richard would turn out to be gay since Richard was five years old. Although he'd tried to erase it from his memory, he could never forget what happened. It was on a weekend. They were reading the Times, and listening to music on the radio when Richard announced he was going to put on a show for them. He went away and after some ten minutes came back wearing Miriam's shoes, a blouse, and some of her jewelry. His lips were bright with her lipstick. He stood in front of them and sang all the lyrics of *Puff, the Magic Dragon*, complete with waving of hands and twirling around. He was very good. He knew the words and sang in tune. When he finished they told him how wonderful he was. But for Alex the fear had been generated.

Mabel and Henry were waiting for them in front of the theater. Henry was wearing his usual silk turtleneck under a blue blazer, complete with shiny gold buttons. Mabel was Mabel, necklaces, rings, and bracelets, sparkling, as well as glittering. They greeted Miriam and Alex with hugs and kisses.

"Just to remind you," Miriam said, "no mention of my biopsy. Richard knows nothing about it."

"All right," her mother said. "I still think you were wrong not to tell him, but so be it. I won't say a word."

It was still a half-hour until the play started, so there was nothing to do but wait in front with the other theatergoers. It was a warm night for October, so the waiting was not unpleasant. Alex noticed that the crowd was mostly forties to sixties, but scattered among them were quite a few younger people, probably friends of the cast. And then his eyes locked with a strikingly handsome black youth who smiled at him. Alex remembered it was Richard's roommate. The young man waved and headed in his direction. He struggled to remember his name but couldn't.

His handshake was firm, his smile dazzling. "Hi Mr. Gunther. JaMarcus Young. You remember me. I'm a friend of Richard's."

"Of course," Alex said.

JaMarcus turned to Miriam. "Hello, Mrs. Gunther. Nice to see you, too."

Miriam introduced him to Mabel and Henry, explaining he was Richard's roommate. "I guess Li Ling is backstage with Richard," Miriam said.

"That's right. And she is so nervous."

"Is she? I thought she was the cool one. How about

you? You must be nervous too, considering you're the one who wrote the play."

"Actually, I am, but I'm trying not to show it."

He excused himself and went back to his friends.

"That's interesting," Alex said. "I didn't know they were all involved."

Miriam gave him a look but didn't say anything.

The Festival was one of those quirky off-Broadway venues. It consisted of three small theaters—one in the basement, one on the main floor, and one upstairs. *Iago's Dance of Death* was upstairs. When the time finally came to go inside, they proceeded up a scruffy staircase, gave their tickets to a young girl with two gold rings in her nose, were handed programs, and shown to their seats. There were fifteen rows of seats with no aisle in-between. The rows were quite long. Their seats were in the middle, which Alex thought would make for an uncomfortable exit if there were an emergency in this potential firetrap. He could just imagine people panicking in their rush to escape.

He and Miriam had gone in first, so he was seated with Miriam on his right and Mabel on his left. He glanced at the program. It was a sheet of paper folded in half. Unlike a *Playbill*, there were no bios, just a listing of the actors and others in the production, along with a few ads from local restaurants. Alex saw that Richard was playing the part of Iago, the lead role. He pointed it out to Miriam. "He's the star. How do you like that?"

"If you'd been interested, you would've already known that."

The lights dimmed and the curtain rose. Four characters were on stage, one of them was Li Ling. Richard wasn't on yet. The play was in modern dress and appeared to be using some of Shakespeare's characters from Othello. But it wasn't Othello. It was a story about a businessman and his mistress, played by Li Ling.

Alex thought the dialogue was uninspiring, and the characters not very interesting. He waited for Richard to appear. This occurred a few minutes later. When he entered, Li Ling and another character had been speaking. They stopped and turned to look at him.

There was a hush. Then Richard spoke. "You lackluster piece of garbage," he said. His voice boomed and filled the auditorium. "You snail. You pusillanimous turd. Come and kiss me."

There was a burst of laughter. The play went on. The dialogue now crackled. The actor's movements were heightened. There was electricity on the stage and in the audience as well. Where before there'd been coughing, rustling noises, now there wasn't a sound, except for occasional snippets of laughter.

The play went on for an hour and a half without an intermission. When the curtain came down there was a brief moment of silence, then an explosion of applause. The curtain opened to show the actors in a row, holding hands. The audience rose and began shouting. As each actor stepped forward, the applause rose. When Richard's turn came, the audience screamed and stamped their feet. They yelled *Bravo* over and over.

Miriam was smiling with tears in her eyes. She and Alex hugged each other.

"Amazing," Alex said. "He was absolutely fantastic."

"What did I say?" Mabel said. "Didn't I say that?"

"Yes," Henry said, the first time he'd spoken all night. "You did say that."

They waited for the audience to leave. When the theater was almost empty, they went out into the aisle and Richard came down from the stage to greet them.

He was still wearing makeup, his eyes lined in black. Miriam grabbed hold of him and kissed him. Mabel had her turn. Henry and Alex shook his hand.

"Well? What do you think?" he said.

"You were fabulous," Miriam said, hugging and kissing him again.

"Absolutely," Mabel said. "I'm a very proud grandmother." She kissed him again, too.

"And I'm an even prouder father," Alex said. Now he leaned forward and put his arms around him. "You were amazing. And the play was terrific. And Li Ling, too. We have to congratulate all of you."

"It's amazing, isn't it?" Richard said. "Never thought we'd get a reaction like that. We're having a cast party in a place around the corner. You're invited, of course."

"We were hoping to take you out to dinner," Miriam said. "But I understand. You certainly want to be with your friends tonight."

"It'll be fun, Mom. The place is called, *Florio's*. I've got to get changed. See you all in a few minutes."

They walked around the corner and found *Florio's*. It was more a bar than a restaurant. It was packed, the bar occupied mostly by men. Alex wondered if this might be a gay bar. The actor's friends were already there. They had taken a few tables in the rear. Alex, Miriam, Mabel, and Henry found a table near them and ordered drinks.

After a while, Richard, Li Ling, and JaMarcus came in. Their friends greeted them with cheers. The noise level rose at a steady pace.

Richard came over and sat with them for a while. "Are you having a good time?" he said.

"I can't hear myself think," Henry said. "But otherwise, it's great."

"Sorry about that," Richard said. "But you can't blame them. We're all pretty happy."

"Don't worry about it," Mabel said. "We're having a great time."

JaMarcus and Li Ling came over and joined them for a while.

Eventually, they said their goodbyes and headed out into the now quiet night. They parted company with Mabel and Henry and walked slowly to their car. Alex took a deep breath. "The air smells so good after all that cigarette and whatever smoke."

"Yes," Miriam said.

On the way home, Alex had a flash remembrance of *Puff, the Magic Dragon*. "Richard is very talented. But more important, he has a phenomenal presence. When he's on the stage you can't look at anyone else."

"Don't you think you're a bit prejudiced?"

"Yes. But I really believe he has it. Not many actors do."

"I hope you're right. At any rate, it was a wonderful evening. I feel quite happy for a change. How about you?"

Alex didn't answer right away. He didn't want to say anything wrong. Finally, he said, "I don't know about happy. But good, yes. I feel very good."

Chapter 31

He was standing on a grate near a subway station. Underneath him, a man marked by the shadows of the iron grating was holding a puppy. He rushed down the steps. The man held the puppy out to him. Instead of a little furry thing, it now had a rat's tail and its open mouth revealed jagged teeth. Alex demanded to know where the puppy was but the man would not answer him. He heard the sound of an approaching train. It was like a woman screaming.

He woke up, registering painfully that the screaming sound was the ringing of the telephone.

"Mr. Gunther?" It was a female voice.

"Yes."

"This is St. Vincent's Hospital."

"Hospital?"

"Yes. Do you have a son named Richard?"

"What happened?"

"Is Richard Gunther your son? I'm sorry but I have to know if I've reached the right party."

Miriam was awake now. She sat up, awareness or terror in her voice. "What is it?"

Alex held up a hand. "Yes. He's my son. I'm his father." His sleep-clouded brain began to clear.

"Your son is in the emergency room in serious condition. We need you to come in and sign some forms."

"What happened to him?"

"I'm not sure. I was told to call. The surgeon wants to talk to you. It's important you come."

"Surgeon? What does that mean? They're going to operate? What kind of operation?"

"I'm sorry. I don't know."

"We'll be there right away. Thanks."

"You're quite welcome." Polite, as if it were an ordinary phone call, then she added, "Come to the emergency entrance."

Miriam was awake now, sitting up, awareness or terror in her voice. "What?"

"Bad. Richard's in the hospital. St. Vincent's. Get dressed."

"What is it? What'd they say?"

"I don't know. She said something about an operation."

"Operate on what?"

"I don't know, Goddamnit. They didn't tell me."

They dressed without speaking. The silence was thick and viscous as syrup. Downstairs Alex said, "I don't even know where St. Vincent's is."

"I've got a Manhattan phone book. I'll look it up." She went into the room that had been made over into her office and came back in a few minutes. "It's in the Village. Seventh Avenue and Eleventh."

"I must have passed it a million times. Never knew it was there."

The sky was a pattern of stars. He got behind the wheel. It was just past four in the morning. The roads were empty. An occasional car would appear, its lights blazing in the darkness, then vanish, and they would be alone again on roads shining from the reflected light of streetlamps. He came to a corner and stopped for a red light, conditioned to do so even though there was no one else in sight. He could hear the whir and click of the lights changing from green to yellow to red on the other side and back again to green on his. He was imagining all kinds of scenarios as to what had happened to Richard. Had he been hit by a car? Had he just collapsed?

Sitting there, waiting for the light, he suddenly said out loud, "What the fuck am I doing?" He drove through the red light and didn't stop at any other as long as there were no cars in sight.

"Did they say anything else?" Miriam said. "That you're not telling me? Is his life in danger?" Her voice was tight.

He drove through the tiled walls of the Midtown Tunnel and unwillingly remembered his dream. He was again running feverishly through the corridors of the subway station. "I don't know who called. I don't know if it was a nurse or someone from the Emergency Room. All she said was a surgeon was involved."

The hospital did not have a parking lot. He found a space nearby. They went directly to the Emergency Room and identified themselves to a woman at the desk.

"Oh, Gunther. Yes. I have some forms for you to sign."

She went to another desk and came back with papers on a clipboard. "Can you sign these please?"

"What are they?"

"Your son has no insurance. If there's a responsible party we ask that you guarantee payment."

Alex signed. "We want to see our son. When can we see him?"

"I have no idea." The woman's attitude suggested that he was rude to have asked the question. "They told me to tell you to wait when you got here. So that's what I'm doing. Now I'm going to call and let them know you're here."

In spite of the hour, the waiting room was crowded. Every chair was taken. There were women with children, older ones on their laps, babies in their arms. There were men, some together, holding hands, one wearing lipstick and eye shadow, many strung out, shivering, eyes sunken into their skulls. They were mixed in color, but all had in common the frozen stares and strained body posture that recognized the inevitability of a long wait.

Alex did not mind not having a seat. In fact, felt better standing because he wouldn't have been able to sit still. But he was concerned about Miriam. "Can you manage without a seat?"

"I think so. Maybe it won't be long."

"I don't know. There are so many people here."

"If only they would tell us something," she said.

"Let's try to be calm. Hopefully, they'll get to us soon."

The woman at the desk was waving her hand at them. She pointed to a man who had come through a door to her right. He wore the white jacket and pants of a hospital uniform, a stethoscope hung around his neck. Even from a distance bloodstains were visible on his clothing. A white turban bound his head rising in swirls to a small peak like soft ice cream. "

"Come on," Alex said. "There's the doctor."

Closer, Alex could see the copper hue that some Indians had in their skin, but over it was a pallor and a weariness in the man making him seem smaller than he actually was.

"I am Dr. Shrdlu," (In the oddly British yet sing-song way he spoke, it sounded like "Shrdlu" to Alex.) "You are Mr. and Mrs. Gunther?"

"Right," Alex said. "What's going on?"

"Your son needs surgery. We need your permission to operate. Your son was unable to give it."

"Operate on what? What's the matter with him?"

"I'll let the surgeon explain. It's better if he tells you exactly what's involved."

"Who are you?"

"I'm the ER resident. Come with me."

They followed him through the door into a large room divided by curtains into cubicles, in each of which was a gurney with a patient on it. Alex didn't pay attention to these people, they were injured, they were sick, but they did not belong to him.

He stayed close to the resident searching for Richard. He saw his roommates, JaMarcus and Li Ling first. They were just inside a partially open curtain to one of the cubicles revealing the angular, movie-star features of Ja-Marcus standing at the bedside. He raced ahead of the doctor and pushed the curtain aside. Richard lay flat, his head wrapped in bandages that extended over his eyes. Alex took hold of the hand which rested limply at his side. The hand was cold and moist. "Richard, it's me. It's Dad." He didn't know if the boy could hear him.

"I think he's asleep," JaMarcus said. "They shot him full of dope."

Miriam had come in and stood across from Alex. She held Richard's other hand.

Alex looked back at JaMarcus and saw that he had tape on several parts of his face and that one arm was in a cast. "God, you too? What happened?"

The resident spoke, as he moved away, "I'm going to get Dr. Mackay. He should be here soon."

JaMarcus said, "We were jumped. A bunch of fag-bashers. From New Jersey probably. That's where they all seem to come from."

"It was terrible," Li Ling said. Her makeup had been marred by tears. There were lines of mascara on her cheeks.

"But why?" Miriam asked.

"For fun. It's playtime for them, beat up the queers. That's what they come to the Village for. Find faggots and beat the shit out of them." He said it calmly, but bitterly.

"The cast party went on well into the night, or morning, I should say. When we came out they were waiting for us. Four of them."

Miriam said, "Didn't anyone try to help?"

"Some did. But these guys were mean-drunk. They were big and they had bats."

"Bats!" Alex said. "Jesus Christ."

"We didn't stand a chance. If the police hadn't come we'd be dead right now. Thank God they left Li alone."

"Did they catch them?"

"No. They got away. Not a surprise."

"Mom?" It was Richard, speaking in a surprisingly clear voice.

"I'm here, sweetheart."

"You know what I see?...I see like shooting stars...pinwheels...it's so beautiful..."

"That's nice."

"I'm...sorry..." Richard said.

Miriam had difficulty speaking. "Don't be silly. You didn't do anything."

"Don't...want to..." his voice weakened and stopped.

"It's going to be all right," Alex said. "Everything's going to be all right."

Dr. Mackay arrived followed by the Indian resident. Dr. Mackay was very tall, perhaps six-six, making the little Indian standing slightly behind him appear to shrink into the ground like a mushroom. The surgeon was wearing the loose-fitting green clothes of the operating room, his head covered with an elastic-edged cap. He was not more than forty with fair skin and blue eyes. His whole being exuded an air of confidence and redemption. "Follow me," he seemed to be saying, "and you will be saved."

"Your son has a detached retina."

"So it's his eyes," Alex said.

"Of course, I'm an eye surgeon. Didn't they tell you?"

"They told us nothing."

"All right then, I'll explain. The blow to your son's head caused a rupture at the back of his left eye. A fluid, known as vitreous humor, has gotten behind the retina. This is not good. We must repair the rupture and keep the fluid where it belongs. I've done it before. Very rarely is there a problem."

"Can you save the eye?" Alex asked.

"That's what we're going to do. He's young, he's strong. Lucky for him the orbit is intact. If he'd been hit at a different spot the sclera might have been ruptured, the eyeball could have been blown out. That would have been a whole different ball game."

"So he's all right otherwise? No broken bones?"

"That's right. What he's got is serious enough."

The resident held out a clipboard. "We need you to sign this authorization as the next of kin."

Alex signed without reading it. The cost of anything didn't concern him now.

"You can go to the surgical floor. There's a waiting room there."

"How long will it take, the operation?" Alex asked.

Dr. Mackay shook his head. "No way to know until we get in there. We'll let you know as soon as we can." He turned and said something to the resident who nodded and said to them, pointing, "See that nurse over there? She'll show you where the waiting room is."

Alex did not want to leave. He squeezed the boy's hand. Miriam leaned over and kissed Richard, caressing his face at the same time.

The nurse took them into a corridor where there was an elevator. She told them what floor to go to and to turn right or left or something like that. Alex wasn't sure what she said and wondered if they would find the waiting room they were looking for.

JaMarcus asked, "Would you mind if we went with you?"

"Of course not," Alex answered quickly.

They found the surgical floor which was quiet and dim, many of the lights turned down or off at that hour. There was no one at the nurse's desk, so they guessed which way to go. The hospital seemed to be occupied by sleeping ghosts. When at last they found the waiting room, Alex dropped onto a vinyl sofa. He could not help thinking how magnificent Richard had been in the play and now there might never be another.

They sat in silence.

Miriam said, "This is the worst part."

"Anyone want some coffee?" JaMarcus said.

"Yes," Alex said, "but there's no way anything's open at this hour."

"Maybe they have some at the nurse's desk." JaMarcus smiled. "They might have *rachmones* on us and give us some."

"You know what that means?" Alex asked.

"Sure. Take pity on you. I know a lot of Yiddish. I grew up in Crown Heights. I was always intrigued by the Hassidim."

"Good. And if you find me some coffee you'll be doing a *mitzvah.* That's the extent of my knowledge of Yiddish."

"How about you, Mrs. Gunther?" JaMarcus asked.

Miriam shook her head.

Li Ling said, "I'll go with you."

The silence continued after they'd gone.

Alex looked at Miriam who sat in her chair, eyes closed. "I have the feeling you knew Richard was gay," he said.

She didn't respond.

"Am I right?"

Without opening her eyes, Miriam said, "I found out a

long time ago."

"How did that happen?"

"Richard told me when he was fifteen."

Alex stood up. "I see. And for some reason, you never told me."

"Richard asked me not to."

"Afraid of what I'd say?"

"Not at all. He didn't want to hurt you. He knew you'd be upset."

Alex began to pace back and forth. "That poor kid. He was right. I would've been. But that was a long time ago. Right now it doesn't seem to mean anything at all."

He got up and went out into the corridor. There were no signs of anyone in either direction. He came back, went to the other end of the room, sat on a straight chair and closed his eyes. They opened again as if they were spring-loaded. He stared straight ahead seeing nothing, his thoughts spasmodic, kicking like a man at the noose end of a rope.

JaMarcus and Li Ling returned, the girl holding a tray with four cardboard containers, steam rising out of them. "Li had to do all the carrying, JaMarcus said. "We got one for each of you but never asked how you take it. So we got one black, and the other has milk and sugar."

"That's fine," Alex said. "We both drink it black, but we'll manage." He asked Miriam, "You want the black?"

She shook her head. "You take it. Right now I don't want anything."

They sipped at their coffee. No one had anything to say.

After a while, Miriam asked JaMarcus if he had any brothers or sisters.

"Two brothers, one sister."

"Older? Younger?"

"My brothers are older, my sister, younger."

He went on to tell her that his sister was a freshman at Mt. Holyoke and that one brother was a lawyer, and the other worked for the city.

"And what about you, Li Ling?"

"I'm an only child. My parents live in Flushing. I grew up there. But I have an extended family. Uncles, Aunts, dozens of cousins."

The room fell silent again, except for a ceiling fixture that buzzed like a trapped fly. They sat apart from each other, avoiding even eye contact, although it would happen inadvertently. It was strange how when it did happen, the need was to break it off immediately. It was as though there was no way to share the anguish each of them felt.

No one else entered the room. Alex opened his eyes, realized he had been asleep, and saw that Miriam eye's had closed, her head slumped forward. JaMarcus, too, was asleep in a chair, black arm in the white cast, but erect as a Nubian caryatid. Li Ling returned his look with a wan smile.

Alex tried to will himself back to sleep but could not. The tension was too strong. He went out and walked through the corridors looking into rooms, seeing the sleeping corpse-like forms of patients. In one room a light at the head of the bed was on and the occupant, an elderly man with a shaved head, stared back at Alex with a look of terror.

Abruptly, he thought of being in the synagogue, light coming in through the high windows, reading in the Book of Prayers. And he thought that if there were indeed a God the Father then he had a curious way of dealing with his children.

When he returned, Miriam and JaMarcus were awake. Dr. McKay was with them.

"It went well," the doctor said. "It was a little tricky because there was somewhat more trauma than I had expected, but he's all tucked away and sleeping like a baby."

"So he's going to be all right?" Miriam asked.

"I don't foresee any complications. We will have to wait and see, right? We don't want to move too fast. Slow and go, that's the way. You people ought to get some rest. He'll be in recovery a while."

"How long?" Alex asked.

"Quite a few hours, I expect."

"Thank you."

The doctor left.

JaMarcus said, "Thank God. What a relief." He wiped at his eyes with the back of his good hand.

Miriam put her face in her hands and began crying. Alex put his arms around her. He thought he could give her some comfort, but her body was as unyielding as a block of wood.

Chapter 32

It was almost seven in the morning. They were going to remain at the hospital but the nurse at the desk assured them that Richard would be in recovery several more hours and that they would do better to return in the afternoon. They were all exhausted.

JaMarcus invited them to rest at the apartment he and Li Ling shared with Richard. They thanked him for the offer but declined. The roommates said goodbye and left.

Alex stood and stretched his arms above his head. "I'm so tired I can hardly function. But I think I ought to go to work. At least, show up. My office is right near here. You don't mind, do you?"

"If that's what you want to do, fine," Miriam said. "I can drive the car home."

Was there something in the manner of her saying it? Or was it something below the surface? Or it was the way her body seemed to stiffen, all the while looking away from him? He didn't know why, but he had the distinct feeling that what had happened to Richard had also managed to effect some kind of radical change in their lives.

He recognized that under ordinary circumstances this was a time when they ought to be with each other, even if they had nothing to say. Being together would mean mutual support, consolation, a way of giving strength to one another to help get through the intolerable possibilities that lay ahead. But he also recognized that their circumstances were no longer the same. The marital glue that used to hold them together physically and spiritually had somehow lost its strength, resulting in a distance between them that continued to lengthen. And this tragedy had done nothing to change it for the better.

"Okay then," he said. "That's what I'll do. That way, I can get back here around noon and see what's going on."

He walked her to the car, which stood next to a No Parking-No Standing sign, somehow without a ticket. Before she got into the car he touched her arm and she turned to look at him appearing quite calm. The strain of the night had produced dark pouches under her eyes, lines creasing her cheeks and worn off her makeup, yet he could still see the lovely young girl she had once been. A burst of sorrow went through him and was quickly gone. "It's going to be all right," he said. "You heard what the doctor said."

Her voice was flat. "Yes. I heard."

She got into the car and pulled away.

He watched until the car disappeared in the traffic, then he began walking to the office.

Chapter 33

He didn't want to tell anyone what had happened but felt he had to explain why he was dressed the way he was, no tie and needing a shave. He told them there had been an accident and about the injury and operation, no more than that.

When he had the chance he told Wanda, with more detail.

"Is he going to be okay?" she asked.

"I think so," he said. "I hope so."

He managed to work—the routine of repetitive tasks was helpful—and the morning passed quickly. In fact, it was Ruthie who reminded him it was almost noon because he had told them he was going back to the hospital at twelve.

He went to Admitting and learned Richard was out of recovery and in a room. He found him asleep and Miriam watching him. She had changed her clothes, done something to her hair, was once again the well-groomed woman he had always known.

It was a semi-private room. Richard was in the bed near the window. The other bed was unoccupied. Alex sat on a hard chair. Miriam was in a larger, more comfortable one at the side of the bed near the window. "How is he?"

"A nurse was here a little while ago. She said he seems to be doing fine. I haven't seen a doctor yet."

"You been here long?"

"Not long." A flat unemotional tone, not looking in his direction.

Alex stared at his unconscious son, bandaged head, IV hooked into one arm, tubes in his nose and mouth, and remembered the infant smelling of baby powder and sour milk he had held in his arms. He could see himself in the middle of the night, his turn while Miriam slept, holding Richard, the warm bottle to his mouth, and watching the infant hungrily suck the nipple. Even though he was usually more than half asleep there was an awareness of how delicious that moment was, an almost sensual feeling of goodness and wholeness that he somehow knew would never be found again.

"JaMarcus was here," Miriam said. "He left a little while ago."

A nurse came into the room, checked the IV, noted his pulse.

"How is he doing?" Alex asked her.

"Everything is normal," the nurse said, matter-of-factly. "A doctor ought to be in soon. You can ask him."

After the woman left, Miriam said, "She could care less."

"Some do, some don't."

He and Miriam sat on either side of the bed. They did not look at each other. There was a connection of sorts, but it was a debilitating one, draining energy from him, creating confusion. He needed to maintain an intellectual distance from their relationship so he could deal with the problem of Richard. He wanted to be rational when a doctor appeared, ask the right questions, pay attention to the answers.

An aide wearing a blue uniform came into the room holding a food tray, looked at Richard, and said," I guess he's not ready to eat yet," and left.

Richard moaned briefly. Alex sat forward on his chair. Miriam got up and put her hand on Richard's cheek. She let it rest there a moment, then sat down again.

"He must be dreaming," Alex said.

"Probably bad ones," Miriam said. "I remember my mother telling me she had nightmares after they took her gall bladder out. She said she was glad to wake up even though there was a lot of pain."

"I hope he's all right," Alex said, and suddenly his eyes filled. He covered them with his hands. He could feel his body shuddering, tried to control it but could not. He took a handkerchief out of his pocket and dabbed at his eyes. He knew Miriam was looking at him, but she said nothing.

Some time later a doctor came in, stethoscope around his neck. He was young, either an intern or resident. He looked at the chart hanging on a clipboard at the foot of Richard's bed. Then he put his stethoscope on Richard's chest for a moment, glanced cursorily at his bandages and at the IV.

"How is he?" Alex asked.

"Stable."

"Is that all you can tell me?"

"Afraid so. It's too early. But everything looks good."

After he left they sat in silence again. Another patient was wheeled in. The curtain was drawn while the patient was lifted into bed, then pulled back revealing the new arrival. There was a mass of curly white hair visible above the covers and two bits of blue that looked them over briefly.

"You think Dr. Mackay is going to come by?" Miriam asked.

"I'll ask. See if anybody knows anything."

He inquired at the nurse's desk and was told they expected him to be there, but of course, they could not tell him when. He walked through several corridors to delay going back. He peered into rooms wondering if he would see the shaven-headed man from the night before, but he did not see him. Finally, he went back to the room.

"Anything?" Miriam asked.

"They expect him. That's all they know."

He sat in the chair again. Looked at Richard, the boy lying flat and unmoving, bandages wrapped around his eyes. The TV was above his head but it wasn't on. He thought about moving his chair and watching it but decided it wasn't worth the effort. Sounds from the corridor drifted into the room, voices, carts being wheeled. The sun sent shafts of light through the blinds. His mind drifted off into memories of another time being in a hospital. He was ten years old. His mother had brought him to visit his father who'd had a gall bladder removed. He remembered asking what a gall bladder was and his mother shushing him and telling him to be quiet and not disturb his father. It didn't bother him because he was used to being told to be quiet by his mother. An aide wearing a green uniform came in and changed the water carafe at the side of Richard's bed.

Alex opened his eyes, realizing he must have dozed off. He yawned and looked at his watch. It was a few minutes before five. "I'm going to call my office," he said.

He asked at the desk if he could use their phone to make an outside call and was told it was ok. When Ruthie answered he explained that he wouldn't be back. Mr. Roth got on and asked him about the Georgian Silversmith's account and how far had he gotten with collecting the twenty-five K owed to them.

"The file's in my desk. They've made two payments of five thousand dollars each. Another one should be due soon. I'm not sure when."

"Okay," Roth said. "Good luck. Hope everything's okay."

Back in the room, Alex said, "Let's go get something to eat."

"I'm not hungry."

"Neither am I. I just need to do something."

"You go ahead. I'll wait here. The doctor might show up."

"You want me to bring you anything?"

She shook her head, her gaze on Richard.

He found the coffee shop, a cold, unappetizing place, partly filled with uniformed hospital workers as well as visitors. All he could think of to eat was a corn muffin and coffee. One bite of the muffin was enough. It tasted like straw. At least the coffee helped.

Back in the room, the time passed slowly. Alex imagined the sand in an hourglass draining particle by particle, one grain at a time. He kept shifting in his chair, trying not to think about what was happening to his son's eyes, hoping that everything would eventually turn out all right.

At just past seven o'clock, Dr. Mackay finally arrived. He was wearing a suit and tie and appeared to be quite different from the man in surgical scrubs. He pulled the curtain between Richard and the white-haired patient. He felt for Richard's pulse and nodded. "As I told you before, the operation went well. His temperature is normal. So far there are no complications. They'll be changing the dressing soon. There's nothing else to do now but wait."

"When is he going to wake up?" Alex asked.

"Soon, probably. It's just the anesthesia. Sleep is good. Nothing to worry about. You folks might want to go home and rest."

After he had gone, Miriam covered her face with her hands.

Alex said, "I want to believe him."

"I do believe him. I've asked around. He's one of the best eye surgeons in New York."

At eight o'clock a nurse came in and said they had to leave.

"Might as well," Alex said. "You must be exhausted."

Miriam stood up and kissed Richard. As they began to leave the room the old man in the other bed spoke, "You're going home now?" His voice was hoarse and there was a trace of an indeterminable foreign accent.

"Yes."

"Good night," he said. "Don't let the bedbugs bite."

"Same to you," Alex said.

The elevator was crowded with both visitors and hospital workers. Two teenagers, who might have been coming from the maternity ward, smiled and high-fived each other while Alex and Miriam stood side-by-side, shoulders touching, enveloped in a fog of weariness. On their way out he asked, "Where are you parked?"

"There's a lot on the next block."

Now he decided this was the time, or maybe he had decided long before. He took a deep breath and said, "Do you want me to walk with you?"

"Why wouldn't you?" She stopped and turned toward him, her look puzzled. But only for a moment. Her eyes grew hard, understanding. "Aren't you coming home?"

The words tumbled out of his mouth, guilt combined with anguish. "I thought you might want a break. Be away from me a while. Maybe it would be better if I went to a hotel."

"What are you trying to say?"

"I don't know. There's so much going on I can't think straight. I have the feeling that you're blaming me for a lot of this."

"For Richard getting beaten up? That's ridiculous."

"Not for that. For being a lousy father. A lousy husband. Not being there when I should have been there."

"It's a little late for that, isn't it? I don't blame you. But if you don't want to come home, fine. I'm too tired to argue." She stepped off the curb, away from him. She became smaller as the distance increased. Then she was gone.

Chapter 34

Nobody pushed him. Why now, he had no idea, it just seemed inevitable. He had jumped off the cliff all by himself and now he felt as if he was still in the air, carried along without direction, like a balloon cut loose by its owner. Consequences? He didn't want to think about them.

He walked back to the hospital and called Wanda from a payphone.

"How is your son?" she asked immediately.

"Doing okay as far as we know." He drew a deep breath. "I want to be with you."

"And I'd like to be with you."

"I mean now."

There was a moment of dead air. "I don't know about this."

"Please. I need you."

"Are you sure you know what you're doing?"

"I'm not sure about anything."

Silence again. Then, subdued, "All right."

He knew she lived in Long Beach. "What's your address?"

She gave it to him.

He took a taxi to Penn Station and had to wait twenty minutes for a train. While waiting he tried to shut down his brain. He didn't want to think about what he was doing.

But on the train ride he could not help himself. It was as if he were being assaulted by a dream, with various images coming out of darkness for a split-second in bright light and then darkness as the next one appeared: Miriam's eyes filled with tears, Richard's bandages, the shaven-headed man sitting up in bed, JaMarcus's handsome face, Wanda...When he thought of Wanda the image did not remain frozen. She moved, stretching, arching her body.

He felt a stirring between his legs and opened his eyes realizing abruptly they'd been closed. Having slept little in the past few days, the motion of the train had put him out. Perhaps it had aroused him as well. He stared out the window into the darkness, unwilling to allow that feeling to continue when his son lay on a hospital bed. It wasn't right, he knew. But he also knew he was fooling himself. What he wanted right now more than anything, was Wanda. He wanted her body. He wanted urgently to be inside her.

She was on the top floor of an elevator building. The elevator was slow, increasing his impatience. It was an old building with an old elevator that rattled itself slowly as it rose.

He rang the bell, his heart pounding, his knees weak. When she opened the door, he didn't see her. He saw a vision, an aura. He stepped in and kissed her hungrily, forcing his tongue deep into her mouth. She was wearing a robe. He pulled it open and saw that she was naked. He put the palm of his hand on her breast and felt the nipple come erect.

She looked into his eyes while her lips curved into a small smile. She led him into the bedroom and undressed him, deliberately taking her time removing his jacket and tie, unbuttoning his shirt, loosening his belt, and unzipping his fly. He closed his eyes feeling the clothes being removed from his body. All the while his desire grew until he could hardly breathe.

He was inside her immediately and came almost at once. "I'm sorry," he said. "I couldn't help myself."

"It's okay," she said.

"I'm not usually a selfish lover."

"Don't worry about it."

He felt no release, only exhaustion.

Wanda said, "Do you want to talk?"

"About what? The man in the moon? How lousy I make love, why I'm here?"

"Either, or."

"No. I don't want to talk."

"Okay," she said.

He closed his eyes and was immediately asleep. He was dreaming again, only this time he knew it was a dream. He was walking on a beach. He was alone and the wind was fierce and blowing sand into his eyes. He tried to rub his eyes to stop the irritation but couldn't manage to do it.

He woke to find his arms stretched out above him. He couldn't move them. Then he realized he couldn't move them because they were tied to the bedposts.

He didn't see Wanda. "What's going on?" he called out.

"You don't have to yell," Wanda said. "I'm right here."

"What are you doing?"

"I'm going to make your troubles go away. At least for a little while."

"I don't think I like being tied up," he said.

"You will."

"What are you going to do?"

"You sound worried," she said.

"Maybe I am."

"Don't be. Everything will be all right. Trust me."

"Do I have a choice?"

She laughed. "I think maybe you should have your legs tied, too. Don't you?"

"No."

"Yes you do."

He watched her go to the night table and open the drawer. She was still naked. He looked at her body and couldn't help admiring how beautiful it was, her breasts full, her ass round and dimpled, her skin silky and glowing, like one of Modigliani's nudes. She came back with foot-long lengths of old-fashioned rope, the kind with fibers that scratched and might leave marks on him like fine cuts. He couldn't help thinking that Miriam might see them, then laughed at himself because it was too late to worry about that.

She made a loop around each ankle and attached them to the front posts. When she finished, she asked him if she had made them too tight.

"No."

"I didn't think so, but I wanted to make sure."

She sat on the side of the bed and put one hand flat on his chest. Then slowly she contracted her hand so that her nails all but punctured his skin.

"Don't draw blood," he said, and he heard the sound of his voice strange and hollow.

"I like blood," she said. She leaned over and began to lick his nipples. After a while, she sucked them, then gently bit, her teeth like the edge of scissors. He could feel himself harden. Some time after that she took him into her mouth.

A long interval seemed to go by before she eventually rode him, quick breaths, making sounds that were uniquely her own. He struggled against the ropes, pulling with his arms, his legs, trying to raise himself higher, trying to get his body in motion to match hers. He struggled to thrust upwards against the constraints that held him back. As he made the effort he could hear the noises he was making intermingling with hers. She moaned as she came, and when he finally did, it was an explosion he had never before experienced.

Chapter 35

Wanda made it plain that his stay with her was temporary. "A few days. A week, maybe. I'm not ready to live with anyone."

He didn't try to change her mind. He was glad of the refuge, temporary as it was. And in fact, he soon realized he was glad it was temporary. He understood from the beginning that his attraction to Wanda had come from some kind of need in him. He knew he was not in love with her. Indeed, in the morning, going to the office together, he could feel guilt descending on him, falling on his shoulders like a soiled towel. He had done it, finally, broken the vow he'd upheld for so long.

He remembered the time he'd been sure Miriam was having an affair. He was selling then. He had quit teaching because it didn't pay enough, her mother letting him know that if he wanted a family, he had to *make a decent living* and teaching science to a bunch of spoiled kids in a private school was not the way to do it. He had not tried to explain that most of the kids were fucked-up, not spoiled and that he got a sense of fulfillment when he was able to get through to one or two of them.

One day he had been in the neighborhood where Miriam worked. He decided to surprise her by taking her to lunch. When he walked in, he learned she was already out, having lunch in a nearby restaurant. They told him the name and where it was.

He found her in a booth with her boss, Mitler. There was a familiarity in the way their heads leaned toward each other, their eyes focused on each other. Then he saw the man's hand move quickly from the table. Had it been covering hers? And it seemed to him they greeted him with too much enthusiasm.

Later that night he'd accused her of having an affair. He'd lost his temper and pushed her so hard she fell. Talk about guilt. The guilt he felt now was mild compared to how sick he'd felt then. He was a monster. He begged her to forgive him. He would love her forever.

A bitter memory. That promise was now a lie. And now, of all times. With his son in the hospital. How insane was that? And what was he going to do about it now? Would it continue? Would he keep seeing Wanda? Should he break it off immediately and confess all to Miriam? How could he, with all that was going on? He'd have to be out of his mind. Then it struck him that was exactly how he felt. Out of his fucking mind.

Chapter 36

When Alex told Miriam he was going to a hotel rather than accompanying her home, her immediate reaction was to be shocked and upset. But because she felt it would somehow diminish her in his eyes, she wouldn't allow him to see that. She'd managed to hold herself together and told him it was fine with her. He could do whatever he wanted, including go fuck himself, but she didn't say that.

After she'd driven only a few blocks tears came into her eyes. And then she began sobbing so intensely she was forced to pull over to the curb. She sat there and cried, her hands over her face, her body shuddering. She was lost, wandering desperately in an unfamiliar place of wildness and terror. It seemed the tears would never end, but gradually the intensity began to wear off, the sobbing slowed, and she began to be aware of what had just happened. When it was finally over she took a deep breath and pulled the visor down to look at herself in the mirror behind it. Her eyes were streaked with red, mascara had run, leaving black streaks. Her skin was pale and gray. I look like an old hag, she thought. No wonder Alex didn't want to be with her.

She used a tissue to pat her eyes and erase what she could of the mascara and resolved to do something about how she looked when she got home.

The first thing she did was strip off her clothes and take a long hot shower. Afterward, she wrapped herself in a towel and rested on the bed. Of course, she knew her looks had nothing to with Alex not coming home. In fact, underneath it all, she shouldn't have been surprised. What he'd done was simply acknowledge to both of them that their marriage no longer existed. What had been so good, so meaningful for twenty years had come to its closing stage.

It was hard to believe that a marriage she'd once considered a fairy tale could end this way. Their first years of marriage had been a honeymoon cliché. Their need for each other was astounding. They made love at every opportunity, in every location, and in every way their imagination took them. When they ran out of ideas they bought the *Joy of Love* and tried all sorts of maneuvers, some of which made them laugh so much they couldn't manage to accomplish them. For a long time, they continued to fuck themselves blind.

In time, of course, the sex slowed down, but what happened was that even though the physical aspect diminished, they became even closer in spirit. Their thoughts and ideas commingled on almost every subject. They liked the same movies, music, friends. The only thing they differed on was their taste in food. She loved sweets. All kinds of desserts and especially chocolate. She always had Hershey's chocolate in the fridge and extras in the pantry so she could have her daily, sometimes twice daily, glass of chocolate milk. Alex, on the other hand loved ethnic food, beginning with bagels and lox, hot dogs, corned beef and pastrami, pickles. Second best was pizza, sausage and peppers, linguini and clam sauce, and third best was Chinese.

She sighed, sat up, and put on her nightgown and a robe. What was the use in reliving the past? She had to deal with her current problems. The biopsy had been a week ago. The results should be coming soon. If it was cancer, would they take her breast, leave her disfigured? It was a distinct possibility, one she'd tried to put off thinking about because it was so distressing, but it wasn't possible. Her mind kept coming back to it, picking at it as if it were a scab.

She opened the closet door with the full-length mirror on it. She took off her robe and nightgown, letting them drop to the floor, and observed her body. She was no longer the young girl with an 18-inch waist. She'd gained some twenty pounds. She had some rolls of fat on her belly, her breasts were no longer thrusting upwards, but they didn't droop too much. All in all, her figure wasn't too bad for a forty-something.

But how would she look with one of her breasts gone and a hideous scar in its place? Or perhaps both breasts might have to go. Would any man want to look at that? Of course she knew there were options like reconstruction and special bras, but that was too gruesome to even think about just now. What she had to do was recognize that it was about time for her to stand up, pull her head out of the sand, and deal with whatever happens.

She closed the closet door, put her clothes back on and went downstairs to the kitchen. She wasn't hungry enough to eat a meal, so she had toast with strawberry jam and a cup of tea. The house was quiet, except for the humming sound of the refrigerator. Occasionally, a car passed by. She felt comfortable in her kitchen. She'd decorated the whole house, but the kitchen was her favorite. There was abundant counter space, pale yellow cabinets, the best appliances, and a pantry. And even though desserts were what she enjoyed the most, she still liked to cook. She did mostly simple meals, but she could also make a more complicated dish like a *coq au vin* or a *boeuf bourguignon*.

Her thoughts returned to her son's terrible experience.

The trauma would probably be with him for the rest of his life. Would his eyes be normal again? She prayed the doctor's diagnosis was correct and all would be well. But nothing was guaranteed.

She thought about calling her mother. It wasn't too late. But what was there to tell her? Nothing new, really, but it might be good to hear her mother's voice, to speak to someone who loved her. Yes, it would be, but she couldn't do it. Once she began to talk, she knew she wouldn't be able to hold back what had happened with Alex. She'd spill everything, and more tears would flow. Her mother would comfort her, and then what? She'd cried enough for one night.

She put the dishes in the sink, turned out the lights, and went back upstairs to try and get some sleep. She took the latest issue of *The New Yorker* with her. She settled herself in bed and tried reading. It was no surprise that she couldn't concentrate. The words had no meaning. Her mind was elsewhere. Scattered thoughts racing like wind-driven clouds, going in all directions, but mostly backward into the past. A rag doll she'd called Molly that she slept with. Her mother taking her to see The Nutcracker.

She remembered the first time she'd made love with Alex. He'd been so tender, she'd begun to cry. He kissed her tears and told her they were salty and got her to laugh. That's when she knew she loved him.

But where was he now? Why a hotel at this juncture? She felt it was quite likely he was seeing someone. A moment of rage flared up. How could he be with another woman with all that was going on?

Miriam eventually fell asleep, but her dreams woke her up several times during the night.

Chapter 37

Alex went to the office the next morning with Wanda. "I'll go in first," she said. "We don't want them seeing us come in together."

She was taking charge, just as she had in bed. He'd liked it there, her domain, but not here, where it should have been his. Still, it wasn't worthwhile to argue. So he walked around the block before going in.

He worked harder than usual, in the hope it would take his mind away from what had just happened with Wanda. He also did not want to think about everything else in his life—Miriam, his father, his mother, Clarice. He did not even want to think about his new unknown sister. All that was nothing but bullshit now. The most important thing in his life was his son. Everything would have to wait on Richard.

He explained the situation to Mr. Roth who grudgingly allowed him to work only half a day.

When he got to the hospital Miriam was already there. She looked tired. Probably hadn't slept well. She made brief eye contact with him then looked away. An arctic chill emanated from her. This did not surprise him, only reinforced the proof of how much he had hurt her the night before. He was grateful that she didn't ask him anything about how his night had been.

Richard slept, hardly moving. He mumbled in his sleep,

the graph on the monitors moved in rhythm.

After more than an hour of doing nothing, Alex said, "How long is this going to go on?"

"However long it takes."

"I know. I know," he said.

Miriam had endless patience. He didn't. Sitting in a hospital room for what seemed like an endless period of time, exhausting and intolerable. He tried to offset the boredom by reading some of the magazines he found in the waiting room. It didn't help because he could only manage a few sentences. He switched to the television and watched game shows, news, sports. The TV was mounted on the wall in a place suited to the occupant of the bed, not to someone in a chair. The combination of boring content and uncomfortable watching, made him get up frequently and walk in the corridors. In fact, nothing helped.

Finally, after more than four hours had passed, he asked Miriam if she wanted to go to the cafeteria with him.

"I'm not hungry," she said, still not looking at him. She hadn't looked at him once all day.

He knew she was angry. He wished she would say something, yell at him, even curse him. Anything would be better than this frozen silence.

"All right then. I'll go. I need to do something."

The cafeteria was filled with hospital workers, some in green scrubs, some in white. There were guests, too. You could tell the difference. The workers were all young, animated, talking to each other. The visitors were wearing civilian clothes and looked as if they wished they were somewhere else.

Alex picked up a ready-made tuna fish sandwich, got coffee from an urn, waited in line to pay the cashier, then sat alone at a table. He ate half the sandwich but drank all the coffee. He went back to the room.

Nothing different happened for the next several hours

until visiting time was over. They went down in the elevator together, neither of them speaking. Outside, Alex said,
"Good night. See you tomorrow."

As expected, Miriam didn't reply.

Alex headed straight back to Wanda's apartment.

Chapter 38

When he arrived at the hospital the next day, Richard's eyes were open and he was sitting up in bed. Miriam was already there, holding Richard's hand.

"Fantastic!" Alex said. "How are you feeling?" He wanted to touch him, kiss him, but Miriam's presence held him back.

Richard tried to smile. "I'm feeling a bit woozy. Got a bit of a headache, but I think I'm okay."

"I see the IV is still going. Is it bothering you?"

"Not really. They told me I need the nutrients they were giving me. But more important, the doctor told me the operation went great. I'm not going to lose the eye. That's pretty good news."

"Great news," Alex said. He didn't add that he was still more than worried.

Miriam said she was going out to call her mother and tell her the good news. Alex said he would do the same and call his mother.

Not long after, Miriam's mother arrived at the hospital accompanied by Henry. He was dapper, as usual, wearing his blue blazer and silk turtleneck.

Alex's mother came in almost at the same time, She was grave, and did not have much to say, but that was not surprising. She signaled for him to join her out in the corridor. "How are you managing?" she asked.

"Okay. How are *you* managing?"

She touched his arm. "I'm trying. But I know how difficult this is for you. Thank God Richard will be all right."

"It's difficult for everybody." They walked to the visitor's lounge. "Come in here for a minute," he said. "I have something to tell you."

After they were seated, he said, "I don't know if you want to hear this, especially now, but before this all happened, I managed to get some information about my sister."

She shook her head, sadly. "I thought you promised you weren't going to do anything about that."

"I know I promised, but I just couldn't help it. I went to see Rudi Emmenthaler. Remember him?"

She nodded.

He told her all that he'd learned. "The woman my father had the affair with. She's Rudi Emmenthaler's wife now. How about that? She was the woman in the diary."

"I really don't want to hear about it."

Alex went on anyway. "But she refused to tell me where her daughter was. Said it wouldn't be fair to her."

"She's right."

"That's what Miriam said."

"Of course. It could even be traumatic for her. I assume they never told her anything. To find out now, after all this time, that your father is not your father. That your mother had an affair with a married man and you're the result. Think about it. How would you feel?"

"I'm not sure."

"Well, I'm sure. It could be a terrible blow."

"Maybe so, but I still intend to find her."

"Son, don't you realize this could have a very bad result? There's no saying what could happen. The whole thing might explode like a bomb."

"I don't see it that way, Mom."

"You've always been a stubborn child."

"In case you haven't noticed, I'm not a child anymore."

"Then act like an adult. And stop this foolishness."

Chapter 39

Wanda lived in an old hi-rise, a one-bedroom, furnished partly with what came out of the house she had once shared with her ex-husband. Her place had a thrown-together look, but it was comfortable, and it was on the top floor, with an ocean view.

The routine continued. Sometimes she would open the door wearing a robe over a nightgown, the lacy bottom of which would swirl at her ankles. Sometimes she wore nothing. She always seemed to have that Sunday morning look, hair tousled, eyes sleepy.

When he put his arms around her, he would nuzzle his face into the soft hair at her neck. He'd take a deep breath anticipating her smell of fresh flowers, like gardenias, either from shampoo or perfume. Immediately, at the first touch of her, he would get hard. She did that to him as if he were still the same horny kid he had been at sixteen, getting stiff every time he passed Marian Shore's house because she had jerked him off once and all he wanted was her hot hand on him again.

On Wanda's bookshelves, he discovered books dealing with astrology and also books of poetry, among them, Emily Dickinson and William Blake, Clarice's favorite poets.

"What's your sign?" she had asked, the first time they were alone in the office.

"Taurus." He had felt her calm stare and a stirring of interest. "What's yours?"

"Aquarius."

"Is that good?" he asked.

"It might be."

He didn't pursue it. He'd always thought astrology was a joke.

Mornings, they ate a breakfast of cold cereal with a cut-up banana or scrambled eggs with toast. They sat at the table in the small dining room and looked out at the ocean. From her window, it was like being on a cruise ship with nothing in sight except water and sky. They watched the surfers, slick black wet suits silhouetted on the glistening water, the bright sun bouncing haphazardly off the waves and the foam.

On the server in the dining room was a framed photo of Wanda's daughter next to the one of her mother. In contrast to Wanda and her mother, the daughter appeared to be plump, with blond hair worn curly and short. She was smiling, standing in front of an ivy-covered wall that was probably her dormitory. The photo of Wanda's mother had been taken when she was a young woman. She had Wanda's oval-shaped face, and the same full lips, but unlike Wanda who radiated sex, her mother looked like a dark-haired Valkyrie, shoulders back, eyes cool and confident as she stared directly into the lens. There was something about the look in her mother's eyes that bothered him. He had no idea why.

"How's your daughter doing at school?" he once asked, to make conversation.

"Made the Dean's List," said the proud mother."

In bed she initiated a course of action he had never before experienced. His body was constantly reminding him of this. After a few days, there were hurts all over him, nicks, cuts, bruises, a residual soreness from the dildo he had let her use.

At night, with Wanda feverishly investigating, charting unfamiliar seas like Vasco de Gama in search of the hidden and unknown, he let himself be taken the way a child gives her hand to an adult, the way a blind person is led by a sighted one. He abandoned himself to the excess, not allowing himself to judge, recognizing the escape it afforded him. He took to it eagerly. He felt he was lucky to have her, the grantor, who brought forth this bounty. He had no problem with the aching power she had over him.

He now existed in a world beyond reality. It was somewhat like being in the middle of a dream. You see things, you do things, but you have no control over your actions. Just as in a dream state everything unfolds before you while you watch and while you willingly, or sometimes unwillingly, participate. Lately, he'd been having dreams of standing in front of closed doors not knowing which one to open.

He'd gone back to the house when he knew Miriam would be out and packed a small suitcase with clothes and toiletries. He was with Wanda all night, went to work, visited Richard in the hospital, then back to Wanda. He did not want to think about what he knew was a bizarre situation. He did not want to think about Miriam but he could not help but think about her. How was she handling being alone? What was happening with her biopsy? Had she heard from the doctor yet? He must make contact with her, even though she'd made it clear she did not want to talk to him.

He had not even given a thought to his sister since this began. Although he tried not to think about what was happening, he couldn't help but wonder why had he chosen this particular moment to allow lust to take over his life.

He didn't have any answers, only that it had seemed inevitable.

Wanda, too, had fallen into this strange routine. She went from their bed to the office, then back to their bed.

The achievement of orgasm consumed them. It was almost a reprise of his first year with Miriam, except that Wanda was more inventive, more interested in the experiment. He made no protest, in fact, he encouraged her. "I don't care what you want to do. Do it."

One time she went to the drawer where she kept the ropes and took out two zippered plastic bags.

"What do you do with those?" he asked.

"Put them on later. In the middle. You breathe your own air. It heightens everything."

"Can't you choke? Asphyxiate? Didn't I read people die doing this kind of thing?"

"They didn't know what they were doing. They went too far. They tried to get more than they needed. Don't worry. Trust me."

"If you say so."

"I haven't hurt you so far."

"Yes, you have."

"But you liked it."

"Yes." He was glad it hurt. He wanted it to hurt.

He closed his eyes and waited for her to begin.

When they weren't fucking they talked. Wanda did most of it. In the middle of the night, under the covers, damp, naked, drowsy but awake, she told him for the first time what her life had been like.

"I married Stanislaus when I was seventeen. I don't know what I was thinking. A way out of the house. Independence. My mother and I were fighting all the time. My father, he stayed out of it. He was a lot older, and let her run the show. Maybe the women in my family are all the same. I mean about men. Stanislaus was ten years older than me. You're twelve years older—"

"Thirteen."

"Same difference. He wasn't a bad guy. He loved me. Too bad I didn't love him.

I got pregnant almost immediately. When Judy was born I felt I didn't need any more in my life. Stan didn't see it that way. I guess gave everything I had to Judy and nothing was left for him. He didn't handle it well. He got sullen. He'd plop himself down in front of the TV after dinner and that was it. Sad on the outside, angry inside. He didn't want to have anything to do with the baby, either. 'What's the matter with you?' I'd say. 'Don't you want to hold her, she's so beautiful?' 'You hold her' he'd say. 'That's all you ever want to do, anyway. Never mind about holdin' me.' He'd act so miserable sometimes I would feel sorry for him and let him make love to me but there was nothing there. He knew it and I knew it.

"Then one night he threw a plate. Out of nowhere. Just like that, he throws it. It smashes against the wall and Judy starts screaming. 'What the hell is that all about?' 'Nothing,' he says. 'I just felt like it.' 'Then you clean it up mister, and if you scare my baby one more time like that, I'm outta here.' And he gives me this wicked little smirk, 'And just where do you think you might go with no money and no job?' I didn't answer because I knew he had me. But that was the end of our marriage. I started putting money away almost the very next day. I took courses in typing and word processing. It took me more than a year before I was able to get a job. The day I got it, I walked out."

They were lying on their backs, hips touching. Now she rolled on her side and put one leg across his. She put one hand on his chest and ran her fingers back and forth.

He put his hand on her leg and gently squeezed. "It must've been tough being a single mother."

"Tough doesn't begin to describe it. I can tell you this: I grew up very fast. Getting a decent job was hard enough, but that was only one small part of it. I had to see that Judy was all right. I left Stan when Judy was five, so she was in kindergarten when I went to work. That helped. It was a full-day kindergarten and they had a daycare afterward that kept her until I got home from work, which was great. But sexual harassment? Forget about it. Every time I began a job I got leaned over, brushed up against, propositioned, and when I complained, was looked upon as a spoilsport. Can't you take a joke? All in fun. Yeah, you bet."

Silence for a while. Then she said, "Do you want to know about the men in my life?"

"I don't think so."

She went on anyway. "There weren't that many. Some of them were nice, most of them were slugs. I always had a hard time telling the difference until it was too late. But one guy...he made a powerful impression on me."

"Who was that?"

"His name was Bill. Just Plain Bill. He was an amazing lover. I was so enthralled I would do anything he asked. So when he started giving me pills, I took them. He got me smoking weed, then I graduated to coke, LSD, heroin. He even found opium. The result was that I was as hooked as any doper you see on the street. All the same, it wasn't all on him, it was on me. I can't explain it. Because it wasn't just the drugs I was addicted to, it was Bill. I was headed South and I knew it, but I couldn't do anything about it."

Alex touched her cheek. "Sounds pretty bad, but I know you did do something about it. Right?"

"Actually, it was Judy. My daughter. She was the one who saved me. She was eleven. Very serious. Very smart. Always got grades in the high nineties. Helped around the house. The kind of kid every mother dreams about having.

One night after Bill left she made me sit down next to her on the couch. Like she was the mother and I was the child. She told me she knew I was doing drugs and that they would eventually kill me. She didn't want to lose me, she said. I was crying my head off. I didn't know what to do. I knew she was right but I was out of control. And then she said that Bill had tried to get her to use. That did it. Hook my baby! It wasn't enough to have me a junkie? I told him never to come around again and I stuck to my guns. He didn't give up easily but I'm a tough cookie when I want to be. So that was the end of Bill. I gave up the drugs. And let me tell you, going cold turkey was about the hardest thing I ever did in my life."

"I've never done that stuff," Alex said. "I can believe it must have been tough."

"Unbelievable. But I did it. I have to admit, though, that I didn't lose my taste for the rest of what he taught me. As you well know."

"So your daughter saved you."

"Yes. And to this day I don't know if she was telling me the truth."

"You mean about Bill?"

"Right. It occurred to me sometime later that she might have made the whole thing up. She was that smart. But I never had the nerve to ask."

"Why bother?"

"Exactly." She moved her hand down to his cock and gently stroked it. "Umm," she said as it began to get hard.

"Yes, indeed," he said. "Umm."

Chapter 40

Richard's condition abruptly changed. High fever. An unexpected staph infection. Delirium. Richard slept again. He did not open his eyes.

Alex had been there during the delirium. Richard had been crying out words, isolated words with no seeming connection "…Hot…dude…sky…JaMarcus…bastards…" His body had writhed under the covers almost as if he were trying to escape from the hooligans who'd beaten him. Afraid he might disconnect the IV, Alex had tried to calm Richard by wrapping his arms around him. But that hadn't worked. He looked at Miriam, hoping she might help. No chance. She was frozen at the other side of the bed, her fingers like talons gripping the blanket, her face deformed by grief.

Desperate, he rushed out to the nurse's desk for help. The sole nurse there had eyes like a raccoon, but when she heard what he had to say, she moved quickly. Once inside the room, she saw what was happening and immediately left to return with a resident. He was young with a straggly beard. He muttered something to the nurse who went out again and came back with a vial and a syringe. After testing the syringe he pushed the needle into Richard's arm.

"What did you give him?" Alex asked.

"Valium. It will calm him down. He has a high fever. That's probably the cause of his distress. We've been giving him a very strong antibiotic. It takes some time before it works. This should help."

Thankfully, he was right. It wasn't long, perhaps only a few minutes before Richard stopped thrashing about and slept peacefully once again.

"Thank God," Miriam said. "I couldn't stand that much longer."

Later, Alex called Dr. Mackay's office.

"Doctor's operating this morning. He'll call you back this afternoon."

No callback. He had him paged at the hospital, got the same story.

They remained at Richard's side all day.

Sometime in the evening Dr. Mackay arrived. He assured them that everything that could be done was being done.

"Exactly what is that?" Alex asked.

"The first thing we have to do is fight the infection. We're giving him an antibiotic that should get it under control."

"We already know that. But why is this happening? You told us everything was fine," Alex said.

Dr. McKay frowned. "The infection came out of nowhere. I'm sorry to say we don't know everything. I wish we did. But we don't."

"So you can't tell us any more than that?"

"Not at this point in time. We'll just have to watch and wait. But all his vitals are good. I'm sure...hopeful, it will all turn out fine."

Several days went by. There was no change. Miriam didn't want to go home. Alex tried to convince her to take a break. She did leave the third day but was back in a few hours. She slept on the couch in the visitor's lounge at night. She began to look like a feeble impersonation of herself. She was pale. Her clothes hung loose and wrinkled. Her cheeks had hollowed and her eyes were receding into her skull.

Alex felt responsible. He realized he could not have chosen a worse time to walk out on her. He knew he couldn't let the present situation continue. He would have to do something, make some changes. If Wanda was hurt, so be it. He didn't feel he had a choice.

Despite Miriam's understandable contempt for him, he tried speaking to her again. "You're not doing yourself any good staying here day and night. And what about your business? Have you thought about that?"

"I have to be here. As for my store, I told the girls what happened. They're running it. I trust it will work out. If they have a problem, they can always call me."

"You won't do Richard any good if you get sick."

"Should I be flattered that you're thinking about me instead of yourself?"

"Look. I'm trying to help. You know I'm just as concerned about Richard as you are."

"You're too late. He's going to die."

Chapter 41

Now he spent his nights in the hospital, too. He had left Wanda's apartment and moved into a cheap hotel on 19th Street near Broadway, a few blocks from the hospital.

His leaving had not been amicable. Wanda said she didn't want him to go.

"I have to be with my son."

"Of course you do. But why does that have anything to do with your leaving?"

He couldn't tell her that for several days he had begun to feel corrupted by his being there. It had actually gotten to the point where he felt that what he'd been doing was so perverted that it might in some way be affecting Richard's recovery. He knew it was foolish to think that way but he couldn't help but think it anyway.

"I'm sorry, Wanda," was all he could bring himself to say. "I just have to go."

"That's not good enough. I need a better explanation."

"I'm sorry. I know I'm repeating myself, but I can't give you one."

He sat in a club chair in the visitor's lounge, Miriam across from him on the couch. An aide had given them blankets. He was not able to get much sleep. The chair was fairly comfortable; trying to sleep in it was another story. His mind was filled with memories of Richard growing up.

He was running alongside Richard holding the seat of the little bike to keep it from tipping, saying, "Don't stop. Don't stop. Keep pedaling. You're doing great." And Richard, excited-scared, falling when he let go, scraping his knee on the sidewalk, crying at either the pain or the frustration. But the boy persisted. He learned. The training wheels came off.

He took Richard out back to play catch and Richard kept dropping the ball and throwing it back with an ineffectual arm motion, the way most girls did. "Throw it like this," he yelled, showing him.

Richard couldn't do it. The boy was trying, but he could not throw the ball the way Alex thought he should.

Alex tried to hide his disappointment. "Okay. Let's forget about it. I can see you don't want to play catch anyhow."

Richard did not answer. The boy went back into the house, Alex following.

They went inside where Miriam, who must have been watching, waited until Richard left the room, then said, "That's great. Another Max Gunther. You want to do to your son what your father did to you?"

"What did I do?"

"You didn't give him a chance."

"Yes, I did. But it's no use. I know he can't help it, but he throws like a girl. Besides that, he doesn't like it. He'd rather be inside with you."

"And why do you think that is?"

The three of them went to the Central Park Zoo. He, proudly held his little boy's hand, lifting him up to see the monkeys, buying peanuts and scattering them for the elephants to pick at with their sensitive trunks.

It was a Sunday. He was home. Richard was ten or eleven, thin, delicate. He'd been outside. He came in, clothes dirty, face wet with tears, snot running out of his

*nose. What happened? "Kids from the next block. They
beat me up. Called me Fishy-Richie, the faggot queen."*

He shuddered. Miriam had to be wrong. The boy had to
live so that he could explain it all to him. He had to know
how much his father really loved him. Richard was not going to die.

Chapter 42

When Miriam first heard about the attack on Richard, she thought she had dealt with it fairly well. Subsequently, his deterioration, along with Alex walking out on her, had caused her own condition to deteriorate as well. She could feel it happening, day by day, a gradual sense of a malaise that seemed to have an inevitability about it that she could only observe at a distance as if it were happening to someone else.

She'd all but stopped eating because even the aroma of food nauseated her. She made do with coffee, tea, and orange juice, or occasionally a slice of dry toast. She no longer bothered with makeup, not even lipstick. Her hair was a mess. When she looked in the mirror she saw an old hag. If it weren't that her clothes were of good quality, she might have been taken for a bag lady.

The one time she'd gone home since the new turn in Richard's condition, she'd called her store to check-in and was gratified to hear all was well. She'd also heard from her cancer doctor. She'd been dreading that call, but in the past few days, had not thought about it once.

"This is Doctor Bromley, Miriam. I have good news for you. What we'd originally suspected in the earlier tests, turns out to have been an anomaly."

"What does that mean?"

"It means you don't have cancer."

She was stunned for a moment. "Are you saying it was all for nothing? The tests, the anxiety? I suffered all for nothing?"

"Miriam, I don't think you understand. As I just tried to explain, the early tests suggested that you might have cancerous cells in your breast. Without the biopsy, we would never have known. I thought you'd be pleased to know that you are cancer-free."

"Of course. I don't know what I'm saying. Of course, I'm happy to hear this. Thank you, doctor. Goodbye."

She hung up the phone abruptly and began to cry.

It wasn't that she didn't feel relief at the news, but it somehow seemed inconsequential in comparison with what was happening to her son. She felt overwhelmed with grief because she was sure he was going to die. And that was something she couldn't bear to think about.

Chapter 43

Alex felt an obligation to put in an appearance at the office. He'd been talking a lot of time off and was sure Mr. Roth didn't like it. He knew he would not accomplish much, but he owed them that.

Of course, the women in the office asked dozens of questions. Wanda was silent, but she didn't have to say anything. Her eyes flashed cold anger.

He told them about Richard's condition. The one personal thing he told them was about his own feelings, his fears, his anxieties, and his disgust with the medical profession.

He heard agreement: "Those doctors, those hospitals. You put your life in their hands every time you go near them. And what do they know? Do they know anything?"

Roth was solicitous. "I know this is tough. But what did I hear? There was a story in the paper about it. He got hit with a bat? Who does things like that? He wasn't hanging out with the wrong people, I hope." The inference hung in the air like virulent dust.

Alex hadn't known the attack had made the newspapers. When he returned to the hospital only JaMarcus was there with Miriam. Li Ling had gone. She'd landed a gig in a sitcom and had moved to L.A. JaMarcus was dressed casually in a sweatshirt and jeans, but he was so strikingly good looking that he always managed to look like a model for Ralph Lauren.

He and Miriam looked up at him as he entered the room. The man with the curly white hair in the other bed smiled at him. Richard lay still. His breathing was thankfully steady, rhythmic.

"Anything?"

"His temperature is down," Miriam answered. "They think they've knocked the infection out."

"So why doesn't he wake up?"

"Nobody knows," JaMarcus said.

"They're hopeful," Miriam said. "They've done all sorts of tests, MRI, cat scan, echocardiogram, God knows what else. There's no reason they can find for his not waking up."

"Maybe the bat did more damage than they knew," Alex said.

"Maybe," JaMarcus said. "I think it might be a good idea to pray a little."

Miriam took a tissue out of her handbag and pressed it against each eye.

"You think God is going to help?" Alex asked.

"It can't hurt to ask," JaMarcus answered.

"*Shema Yisrael,*" the man in the next bed intoned, "*Adonai Eloheiynu. Adonai Echud. Baruch sheim kevod malchuto leolam vaed.*" He smiled at them. "I couldn't help hearing. I hope you don't mind if I pitched in a little."

"No," Alex said. "Thanks for your concern."

"Don't mention it."

Alex went out of the room and walked to the lounge. He sat in a chair and closed his eyes, rubbed them with his fingers.

He opened his eyes to find JaMarcus's hand on his shoulder and his face close enough to see the red veins in the eyeballs. "You were moaning."

"Was I? Sorry. I usually try to keep my moaning to my-self."

JaMarcus sat in a chair by his side. "Do you mind if I stay here?"

"Of course not."

Silence again.

JaMarcus said, "I want to tell you something. I hope you won't take it the wrong way." The skin was taut over his cheekbones and had a sheen as if it had been newly waxed.

"Try me."

"I care about your son." He paused, then took a breath. "I care about him a lot."

"I know that."

"What I mean is, I love him. I don't mean to shock you, but that's the simple truth. I care desperately about what's happening to him. But no matter what the outcome, I am not going to leave him. I want you to know that. I am not going away, even if it means I have to be a nurse the rest of my life."

Alex recognized how difficult it must have been for Ja-Marcus to talk to him. "Richard is lucky to have you," he managed to say, although his voice broke.

After a while, he and JaMarcus went back to the room and found Miriam asleep in her chair. Her head was tilted at a severe angle from her body, her mouth was open, her arms drooped over the arms of the chair. Mewing sounds occasionally came out of her as she breathed. She looked so uncomfortable that he moved closer to see if he could help her somehow, perhaps with a pillow. When he closer to her he saw that in the past few weeks she had aged more than he had realized. Impulsively, he put his hand out to touch her.

Her eyes opened. She sat up. "What are you doing?"

"Nothing. I thought I saw something."

"What?"

"Nothing. Nothing." Moving back. "Forget it."

"I fell asleep. Was I snoring?"

"No. But you looked uncomfortable. You probably have a stiff neck."

She rubbed the back of her neck. "You're so right."

JaMarcus said, "I've got to go. I'll be back later."

"Thanks for being here," Miriam said. "I'm sure he feels it...your presence."

When he had gone, she looked at Alex, "Don't you have somewhere to go, too?"

"No."

There was no place to go, nothing to do but remain there, in that hospital room, watching, waiting, hoping. He might even try praying.

Chapter 44

Richard's comatose state remained the same. It had been explained to both him and Miriam that this had come about because of an unexpected staph infection. Now it occurred to Alex that the staph infection could have happened because of negligence. Of course, he couldn't prove it. But that didn't mean he didn't have any leverage.

He decided on his own that the least he could do was to get Richard moved into a private room. He called Dr. McKay, who said he had no authority to make that happen and that Alex should get in touch with the administrator of the hospital. He gave him the name, Quincy Boylan.

Alex reached him on the phone, introduced himself, gave the information about Richard's condition, and told him what he wanted.

The administrator's response was neutral. "Give me some time to check this out. I'll get back to you."

"I expect to hear from you soon. I'm in my office. You can reach me there." He gave him the number.

A half-hour later, Alex got his return call. "I looked into it, Mr. Gunther. I'm afraid your insurance doesn't cover a private room."

"I don't care about that. I want him moved. If I have to pay I will. But let me point something out to you. I think there's a question of liability here on the hospital's part.

My son has gone into a coma after a routine operation. That brings up a lot of questions and options. I haven't talked to a lawyer yet because I haven't decided whether or not to go that route. But I do think it would be in your best interest to do whatever is necessary to help my son recover."

There was dead silence for a moment. "Let me look into it," the administrator said.

Later that day Alex was informed by administrator Boylan's secretary that Richard had been moved to a private room on a different floor. He felt good but was in no mood to celebrate. It only indicated that he was probably correct there'd been negligence.

Richard's new room was like a hotel room when compared with where he'd been. It had good-looking furniture, comfortable chairs, even a desk. There were two windows overlooking the street that allowed sunshine to flow in. Richard was still hooked up to the IV and a monitor, its green and yellow lines zigzagging across the screen in a steady rhythm.

At first, doctors and nurses, none of whom they knew, kept entering the room, looking at Richard's chart, sometimes checking his pulse, lifting his eyelids, listening to his heartbeat. They ignored Miriam and Alex, and JaMarcus, if he was there. Dr. McKay dropped in occasionally and explained the visitors were students and residents who had heard about Richard and wanted to see him as part of their studies.

One doctor actually spoke to them, introducing himself as the anesthesiologist, and assuring them that his procedures had been nothing less than perfect, that what had occurred was simply baffling to the entire staff of the hospital, and that all that could be done was being done. Alex suspected he had been sent by Mr. Boylan.

He and Miriam had given up sleeping at the hospital. It

had not helped, and the road ahead seemed a long one.

The hotel room he stayed in had become a punishment box. He was suffocating. He felt as if he were in prison. At night he opened the window as far as it would go. He pushed his head out. He could not see the sky because of the buildings. The air was moist and chill and full of soot and the fumes of traffic. In spite of that, he breathed it in hungrily.

One morning he woke up at five o'clock. He had lain on the bed all night with his clothes on, the TV flickering, occasionally dozing, then coming awake again. He took a hot shower, put on clean underwear and a fresh shirt. The pants and jacket were the same ones he had been wearing when he had left Wanda's. He had not considered how long he was going to stay in the hotel.

He called the hospital and got the usual answer: nothing had changed. He put his things in the small valise, took the elevator down to the lobby, and checked out.

Without considering why he was doing it, he was at the office before six. He went to his desk, got his father's diary out of the lower drawer where he had last put it, locked it up again, and headed for the subway.

There were masses of people underground at this hour. They moved with speed and determination streaming around him in all directions giving off a humming sound like a swarm of bees. He felt himself being pushed and shoved. He clutched the diary against his chest with one hand and held on to the valise with the other.

On the edge of the platform, he unwillingly inhaled the odor of unwashed bodies and overly strong perfume. He looked down at the gleaming rails. He thought of his boss Roth and his job. Going nowhere. Little satisfaction. No appreciation. Why didn't he get out now while he still could? Go back to teaching. He wondered if he could do it anymore.

The crowd was thick behind him. He remembered the story on TV about a man accidentally shoved in front of a train and killed. What a laugh if he found himself suddenly pushed onto the tracks. Would he struggle to save himself, or would he accept it as destiny? They would probably say he had chosen to do it. It would even be historically accurate since the tendency was probably in his genes, the evidence provided by his sister.

He looked into the tunnel. At first there was only the blackness and then suddenly there were lights propelling forward. A phrase from the Bible came to him...'more bitter than death'...The lights at the top of the car were like two searchlights, swaying with the motion of the train. He felt dizzy, and thought he was going to fall. He could see the motorman in a small box of yellow in the darkness, his face blurred like a bad photograph.

There was a rumble, then a roar and the train was there, doors opening with a hiss. He stumbled into the car, relieved, and stood pressed against a pole until he got off.

In Penn Station, at the LIRR waiting room he bought a container of coffee that turned out to be so bitter, it was all but undrinkable. He had to stand again until the change at Jamaica where he was finally able to find a seat. The ride to the Centre Avenue station in East Rockaway would take forty minutes. He put the valise up top but held on to the diary.

He walked to the house, anticipating that Miriam would not be there when he arrived, because she would already have left for the hospital. He was glad to see that her car was not in the driveway.

He unlocked the side door that led to the kitchen and put the valise and notebook on the kitchen table. He stood there a moment and listened to the silence of the house. He felt like an intruder as if he didn't belong here anymore.

The refrigerator compressor came on. It was an old

machine that labored all the time. They had talked about replacing it but had never gotten around to it. He realized now it was because in the last few years he could not get himself to make a decision about anything. Then he heard the oil burner in the basement start up. It was comforting, reassuring to hear these sounds. He sat at the table and thought about what he should do next.

A car pulled into the driveway. He looked at his watch, saw that it was just eight o'clock, and realized he had miscalculated.

Miriam came in carrying a brown paper bag. She saw him immediately but said nothing. She put the bag down on the countertop and removed its contents, a coffee container, and something wrapped in white paper.

"You go out for coffee?" he asked.

"It's easier." She got a plate out of the closet, unwrapped the paper, and placed its contents, an English muffin, on the plate. Then she brought it to the table along with the container and sat across from him. "Do you want some?"

He shook his head.

"Sure? I'm not that hungry."

"Neither am I, but thanks anyway."

She shrugged and began to eat.

Miriam had returned to herself this morning. She was once again fully made up, well-groomed, good-looking, and efficient. She wore a navy suit with a cream-colored blouse that had ruffles at the neck. He watched her bite into the muffin and drink from the container, her freshly painted lips leaving a red semicircle on it. She looked back at him giving no indication of what she was thinking or feeling.

Miriam had always been strong. Her father had died young. Her mother was the kind of person who distanced herself from anxiety. If there was a problem, her mother would rather not know about it. Miri had been the grownup in their household.

Now, Miri had had to deal with what you might call, a situation. What was this so-called situation? A tragedy, a life lesson, a sitcom, a blip on the learning curve? It was certainly one full of shit, and she'd had to deal with it all by herself. Unsurprisingly, she had done just that.

Miriam patted her lips with a napkin. "Do you want to tell me what you're doing here?"

"I was hoping I could stay awhile."

"It's your house as well as mine."

"That's nice of you."

"Not really. I have no right to keep you out. Even if we start divorce proceedings, I understand you have a right to stay here."

"Who said anything about a divorce?"

She stared at him for a long moment. "Come on, Alex. We don't have a marriage anymore."

"I know it hasn't been good for a long time. But that doesn't mean we have to give up on it, does it?"

"What are you suggesting?"

"Counseling?"

"I think it's too late for that. I don't think anyone can find a way to repair this."

"Well, we don't have to do anything right away, do we? Can't we wait? Let's concentrate on Richard for now."

He searched her eyes for a sign of understanding, not expecting compassion. "I won't bother you while I'm here. I'll try not to get in your way. I thought I could use Richard's old room."

"I guess that'll be all right," she said.

"Good. I'm glad we worked something out, at least."

She pointed at the things he had put on the table. "I see you're still carrying around your father's notebook. That's it, isn't it?"

He nodded.

"I don't see that it's done you much good."

The phone rang. She got up to answer it. "Mr. Roth, how are you?"

He shook his head and signaled with his hands, then mouthed, "I'm not here."

"No, his condition hasn't changed. But all the signs are good. We're trying to be optimistic…Alex isn't here. He's probably at the hospital…" She listened for a while, then said, "Of course, I'll give him the message. I understand. Thanks for calling." When she hung up, she said, "He's mad as hell and he's not gonna take it anymore."

"Fuck him."

"He says he understands you're upset about Richard, but your job is important, too. Things are going to hell in a handbasket there. Those are his words."

"They would be."

She took her plate, put it into the dishwasher, and put the container and napkin into the trash. "I'm going to the store and then back to the hospital."

"I called earlier. There's no change. I'll be there later."

"That's that, then," she said. As she was going out the door, she said, "Oh, by the way, The doctor called about my biopsy. Turns out I don't have cancer after all."

Before he could say a word, she had gone.

What a relief it was to know something good had finally happened. He allowed himself the luxury of feeling something enjoyable for a change.

He went up to Richard's room, put his valise down, and sat on the bed. Nothing had changed. The same posters of David Bowie, Pink Floyd, and Marlon Brando still stared out at the world.

He found himself holding the diary. He opened it casually, not wanting to read it at this time. He read a few lines, then skipped to another page, read a few lines, and skipped again. Then, because he couldn't help himself, went back to the beginning and read it straight through from beginning to end. For what, the hundredth time? No matter. When he was finished, he ended up feeling the way he had the first time he'd read it. Despite all that was going on, he had to find his sister.

Chapter 45

In the days and weeks that followed, Alex realized that the human mind and body have the extraordinary ability to adjust to anything. It wasn't a great adjustment, he wasn't dancing in the aisles, but he was able to cope. That was enough.

He and Miriam faced the fact that Richard was in a coma, and that there was no way of knowing if he would ever come out of it. While in the hospital they talked to Richard, touched him, and tried to behave as if he were responding. They were told by the staff these were beneficial things to do, that the sound of their voices might be getting through to him.

Richard lay still, tubes attached, one to an IV, another to a monitor on the wall behind him, its green lines marching in an endless parade to nowhere. He was clean-shaven, shaved on a regular basis by the aides, but it was obvious he had lost weight. His face had become leaner, his cheeks hollowed out.

Life outside the hospital went on in an almost normal way. He had worked out an arrangement with Miriam. They lived in the same house, but their interactions were formal. Alex found that by following a routine he could do his work efficiently.

Occasionally, he would be startled, realizing he had drifted off. It could happen at home, or while commuting, or finding himself sitting at his desk with a pen in his hand in the middle of writing a note. There were thoughts of his father, the diary, Clarice, and the waste of her life. Miriam and Wanda were often there. It was difficult to shake these meanderings off and get back to work but he managed it.

One day Wanda left a note on his desk requesting he meet her for lunch at the diner they'd been to before. He didn't want to go. He knew she was going to try to pressure him about their relationship.

When he arrived she was already sitting in a booth. She was wearing a dark blue suit with a cream-colored frilly blouse. She was a very good-looking woman, always well dressed, carefully made up, her long brown hair, shining, as always. She didn't smile or greet him.

He sat opposite her and ordered coffee.

She said, "Aren't you going to eat anything?"

"I'm not hungry."

The waitress came with his coffee and Wanda's order, chicken salad. Alex waited until the waitress left. "Now what's this about?"

"You know what this is about. Us."

He sighed. "Right now, there is no us. I tried to explain that to you. I have my son to think about. That's all I can handle."

"You know what I think?" She stared at him, her eyes like stones. "I think you're using it as an excuse to break up with me."

"That's nonsense. If I wanted to break up with you, I'd just do it. I don't need an excuse." He'd spoken the truth, but the moment the words were out of his mouth, he regretted them. Maybe he was too harsh.

"So then, where are we? How long is this separation going to continue?"

"I don't know. Remember, I told you when I moved out that I needed to concentrate on my son. That hasn't changed. I have to wait until my son gets better. Then we'll see."

"What is there to see? It's quite simple. When he recovers, are you coming back to me, or not?"

He shook his head. "Aren't you forgetting something? Weren't you the one who said you didn't want it to get too serious? That is was all about sex? What happened with that?"

"That was before. This is now. I decided I want you in my life."

"I don't quite know what to say to that. I'm really flattered, Wanda. I didn't realize you felt that way at all." He picked up his cup and took a sip of coffee. "Look. I'm trying to be honest with you. The truth is, I don't know what's going to happen. I don't know how long this thing with Richard is going to go on. I don't know how I'm going to feel when it's all over. I'm sorry. I know that's a shitty answer. But that's all I can tell you right now."

Wanda stood up and retrieved her coat and pocketbook. "In that case, you can go to hell." She walked away before he could say anything.

He remained where he was for a while. He hadn't expected anything like that from her. At the same time, he was surprised to be having mixed feelings. He felt a bit of relief, and at the same time a feeling of guilt. Had he treated her that badly? He didn't think so. He'd never promised anything. But was that what he really wanted? To be free of Wanda?

He left the restaurant and went back to work. He was confused. He knew that much. At the same time, he had a right to be. There was so much stuff going on. He had no clue about his sister. He couldn't follow up on that by going back to Rudi Emmenthaler and his wife. There was no doubt they would have nothing to do with him after what happened the last time he was there. At home, he and

Miriam managed to get along, although they rarely talked. A truce had been declared, unspoken, uneasy, but a truce.

One day Miriam told him she had been contacted by a support group.

"You mean there are that many people in comas that they have support groups for them?"

"Apparently. Do you want to go?"

"No. Do you?"

She shook her head. "I'm not ready."

"I know. I feel the same way. I don't want him to be one of them. I don't want to be in a group of victims. It's like admitting he's never going to come out of it."

They spent weekends at the hospital. JaMarcus was there, too, his strong presence welcome. They were glad he was there, but they rarely stayed in the room at the same time.

Sometimes there were all three of them, sometimes two, sometimes one. Each took turns talking to Richard.

Once, JaMarcus called out, "He squeezed my hand. I felt a response." He smiled, teeth dazzlingly white in contrast to his dark skin.

"You're sure? You weren't imagining it?"

"I'm sure of it."

Miriam said, "I thought I saw his eyelids move a few times, but I didn't want to say anything. I wasn't sure if they really moved."

"We'll keep trying," Alex said. "Maybe we *are* getting through."

The man with the curly white hair who had shared the room with Richard stopped by. He was being discharged. He said he had come by to offer his best wishes.

"I will pray for him in the synagogue," he said. "I will ask my whole congregation to pray. I am sure God will hear us."

"Thank you," Miriam said. "It's very kind of you."

"Kind shmind," he said. "This kind of *tsouris* nobody needs."

After the man left, Alex said, "I'm going out for a while. I'll be back later."

He left the hospital, walked one block to the subway entrance, went down the steps, and got on the train heading to Brooklyn, He had to change at Court Street for the BMT line that would take him to the Kings Highway station, the one he'd used for the visit to Rudi. It was no surprise to see the stores, the traffic, and the grimy litter of the commercial street. He left that behind and began the half-hour's walk to where he was going. He walked through neighborhoods that he thought must have been built by someone who adhered to the architectural design called cookie-cutter. On block, after block, each house was the same two-story Cape Cod with red brick facing, a one-car driveway, and a small plot of garden, most of which were enclosed with cyclone fencing. The shrubs were done in geometric squares, rectangles, and rounds.

He found the place without difficulty. This building differed from the others on the block in that there was no shrubbery, the building taking up the entire lot. It was plain on the outside but Alex remembered the beauty of the sanctuary on the upper floor. The bronze plaque with the name, Congregation Shaare Tefilla, had a green patina, he hadn't noticed before.

He pulled the door handle but the door didn't open. He pulled it again but it still didn't budge. He grabbed the handle with both hands knowing he was being ridiculous and pulled as hard as he could. After two backward lunges, he gave up.

He looked up and down the street. It was early afternoon. The street was empty. There were no people, there was no sun. The gray clouds and scattered autumn leaves gave the place the look of a deserted stage set. A curtain moved in a window across the street. Someone was watching him. Immediately, he crossed over to the house where the curtain had moved and rang the doorbell. No one came to the door. He put his finger on the button and kept it there. He could hear a loud angry buzz.

Finally, the door opened and a woman appeared. "All right, all right. What's the emergency?" She was a heavy woman, wearing a brown bathrobe tied with a multi-colored sash. Scattered about in her hair like snares were a series of bubblegum pink plastic curlers. On her feet were enormous purple and white sneakers. She looked at him without smiling. "You're the person trying to break down the door to the shul?"

"I wasn't trying to break in. I was trying to get in. Do you know where the people in charge might be?"

"What people? There's the rabbi and the *shammes* that's all."

"Isn't there a president of the congregation?"

"That nudnick. I wouldn't put him in charge of a chicken."

"Do you know how I can get hold of the *shammes*?"

"Mr. Natterman?"

"I don't know his name. But he's a…he's small."

"That's him. He lives right down the end of the block." She pointed. "Number eleven. This side of the street. You could try there."

"Thank you."

"What's so important, may I ask, that you have to get into the synagogue? Services are over for today."

Alex hesitated for a moment, then he said, "I was there a while ago and I left something behind."

He walked down the block to number eleven and rang the bell.

In a moment the door opened. "Well, well," Mr. Nat-terman said, in his melodious baritone. "Look who's here. This is a surprise."

"Hello. I see you remember me."

"Of course. The man I thought was a burglar and in-stead turned out to be a student of architecture."

"You're making fun of me."

"Maybe, perhaps. Just a little. Don't worry about it. It's in my nature." He stepped back. "Come in."

"I don't want to bother you."

"No bother, no bother."

Alex stepped inside to find himself in a narrow room that ran the width of the house and might once have been a sunroom. There was white wicker furniture, red cush-ions; the floor was covered by an ornate Persian rug. Now Alex had stirrings of doubt. What was he really doing here? What did he hope to accomplish?

"Take a load off," Mr. Natterman said. He sat in the only chair that was not wicker. It must have been made for him because his feet touched the floor.

The little man no longer looked like a frog. Perhaps the color of his skin had changed, although it was still heavily pockmarked; or maybe, perhaps, as Mr. Natterman him-self might say, because he wore a sport shirt and corduroy pants. At any rate, the only things unusual about him now were his height and his beautiful voice.

"So what can I do for you?" he asked.

"I had an idea. Maybe it's a crazy one. But I wanted to get into the synagogue again."

"What for?"

"It's hard to explain."

"Try. I got better things to do than open up the shul every time somebody gets it in his head he wants to take a look at it."

"It's not to look at. It's personal. I thought it might help."

The little man shook his head. "Not good enough."

"Mr. Natterman. Please! Listen to me!"

"How do you know my name?"

"A lady down the block. It's important. I'll make a contribution."

"You want to bribe me?"

"Of course not. But I'm sure the Temple could use the money."

"Certainly. What religious institution doesn't need money? Especially a little shul like ours. But in this case, I have the feeling you're trying to buy me off, and I don't like it."

"That's not it. I'm looking for any help I can get."

"I remember you told me you had no faith. You said you were an atheist. So what are you going to get in a shul? The rabbi isn't there. There's nobody there but God."

Alex began to laugh. "That's very funny." He tried to stop but found he could not.

"Okay. It's not *that* funny," Mr. Natterman said.

The laughter continued. Tears came out of his eyes. He began to gasp and make wheezing noises.

"All right, already. Enough. *Genug.*"

Alex waved his arms. He could not get enough air into his lungs. He pointed to his mouth.

Mr. Natterman asked, "What can I do?"

Alex managed to get one word out, "…water…"

The little man ran out of the room and quickly returned with a full glass. He helped Alex hold the glass and together they were able to get him to swallow some of the water. It worked. Alex inhaled deeply several times.

"Thank you," he whispered.

The *shammes* sat across from him. "You frightened me."

"I frightened myself. That never happened to me before."

"Maybe you should see a doctor."

"I get it. You mean a doctor for the head?"

"You might put it that way."

"That won't help."

"So what will? Sitting in a shul for ten minutes? I believe in God, but I don't believe in miracles."

Alex didn't answer. He looked down at the elaborate swirling patterns of the rug. They seemed to be trying to tell him a story. "Neither do I. But I'm looking for one, anyway."

"Is it so bad?"

"My son is in a coma. He's never going to come out of it."

"Shah! Pooh, pooh, pooh," he said, using the old superstition. "Don't say such a thing."

"I can't help it. That's what I keep thinking."

"All right," Mr. Natterman stood up. "Come. We'll go to the shul. Maybe it will help. Hurt, it can't. In the meantime, I have something for you." He went out of the room and came back with a small book bound in black. He gave it to Alex.

"What's this?"

"A Bible. From me to you. Give it a glance while you're sitting in the sanctuary."

"That's really kind of you."

"Think nothing of it. Maybe, perhaps, you might find something in there that will help. Who knows?"

Chapter 46

Alex went up the stairs into the sanctuary and sat in a seat in the middle of a row, the Bible Mr. Natterman had given him, in his hand. The sexton had not switched on any lights. There was no need because daylight came in through the massive panes of glass in the roof. Because there was no sun the light that filled the space was gray and cold. The building was cold as well.

He looked around, observing once more the beauty of the pale wooden walls, the carving of the Lion of Judah, the inlaid mother-of-pearl on the arc that contained the holy writings of the Torah.

He closed his eyes and waited. He did not know what he waited for. Maybe for a feeling that might help in some way, or maybe a voice speaking to him the way God spoke to Charlton Heston by way of Cecil B. DeMille.

Alex waited for that voice, any voice. He waited for some feeling to come over him. But other than the sound of his own breathing, there was only silence. And what he felt was only the chilled air.

He opened his eyes and turned the pages of the book in his hand. At the beginning was a list of the order of the "Books" that made up "The Holy Scriptures"—Genesis, Exodus, Leviticus, and so on. He had always thought he understood the meaning of Genesis and Exodus, self-evident really, but never the meaning of other parts of the

Bible, like Leviticus, Numbers, Deuteronomy. He had never been interested enough to learn anything about them.

Now he looked at the first sentence of Genesis: *"In the beginning God created the heaven and the earth."* That was familiar. A pleasant fable, a man with a full white beard creating the whole shebang by holding out his hands like a magician and saying, "Abracadabra."

He turned pages and came to the part about Noah and about God telling Noah what to do and how to do it. No hesitation on either side. God commands. Noah obeys. Build the ark, so many cubits, so many stories. Everything outside will be destroyed because it is corrupt. Talk about judgmental. This is a God that is never satisfied with anything.

Alex continued to read and as he did he found that he was skipping less and reading more. The words, the structure of the sentences, the language had a rhythm and a narrative force that was compelling. He came to the story of Abraham and Isaac where God tells Abraham: *"Take now thy son, thine only son Isaac, whom thou lovest, and get thee into the land of Moriah, and offer him there for a burnt offering upon one of the mountains which I will tell thee of."* And of course, the old man did it. A hundred years old but never questioned the voice of God.

What kind of bullshit was this? What kind of a God was it that would demand such a sacrifice and what kind of father would submit to such a demand? Suppose he was put in that position. A voice comes out of the night and says to him, *"Listen to me. Tell the doctors to turn off the machines that are keeping your son alive. Don't ask me any questions, just do as I say, and I'll make the rest of your life good. Your childhood memories will be full of love and happiness. Everything between you and your wife and your girlfriend will be worked out satisfactorily. Your life will be clean and pure and fulfilling. How's that for a deal?"*

Of course, God wouldn't do that. He doesn't make deals. He just tells you what to do and you do it, no questions asked. If any good comes out of it, that's your blessing, your reward, but it's not in the contract. You think Abraham knew God was going to stop him at the last minute from killing his own son? No way.

He stood and walked up and down the center aisle. It wasn't happening. What he had hoped for, some sort of peace, a kind of understanding, a feeling of release, of acceptance, a sense of direction at least, any one of these would have been a help. But none had occurred.

The light in the sanctuary had grown dimmer making objects indistinct. He looked up through the skylight and saw black clouds migrating restlessly like herds of cattle, enlarging, diminishing as they moved. It would no longer be possible to read without artificial light. It didn't matter. He wasn't going to read anymore. There were no miracles to be found, not in the Bible, not in the place where Bibles belonged.

Downstairs Mr. Natterman sat behind his desk. "So?"

"I want to thank you. For the Bible and for letting me in again."

"Think nothing of it. If you'll pardon me, you don't look so good."

"I don't feel so good."

"You know, I'm not a rabbi, but I'm a very good listener. Maybe you would feel better if you had someone to talk to."

"I wouldn't know where to begin. But I have a question for you."

"Ask."

"Where are the answers?"

"Answers to what?"

"I thought up there, with all that holiness, the Torah, the Bible, the Eternal Light, all the rest of it, I thought I would find answers."

Mr. Natterman held out his hands, palms up. "What can I tell you? There are no answers, really. Only questions." He got up and came around the desk. "I know what you're thinking. Philosophy you don't need." He reached out and grasped Alex's hand. "I hope everything will be all right with your son. I will ask the rabbi to say a *mishebarach* for him."

"I don't know what that is, but thanks anyway."

"A prayer. For his recovery." He shook Alex's hand. "And maybe, perhaps, someday you will also find those answers you are looking for."

"Yeah. Maybe, perhaps."

When Alex stepped into the street the air had become much colder, the sky rapidly darkening into night. The building behind him was a refuge for believers. Maybe even for semi-believers. But for a non-believer like himself, there was no refuge.

He looked up and saw that the clouds had vanished. Stars were beginning to appear. They would soon form their glittering patterns. Clarice's stars, the ones she had believed in, the same ones she had charted for herself and for him.

Chapter 47

When he arrived back at the hospital he went up to Richard's room and found him alone. He guessed Miriam and JaMarcus might have gone for something to eat. He was glad they were not there, pleased to be alone with his son.

He closed the door and sat next to the bed. He put the Bible on the table next to the bed. He looked at the monitor's green lines parading in close order drill, observed the slow dripping of the IV's fluid. He inhaled the subtle odors of chemicals and fear that was as much a part of the hospital as its rooms, its nursing desks, its shining floors.

Richard slept. He was as still and silent as marble, the almost perfect features of his face as beautiful as Michelangelo's David.

The room was in semi-darkness, the only light coming from the fixture behind Richard's bed that threw its glow upwards towards the ceiling.

Alex began to feel the tension that had been driving him gradually dissolving. This was much different than how he had felt in the Temple. He'd gone there in a vain effort to find some kind of spirituality, but it hadn't happened. Or might he have been wrong? Perhaps something had happened there. Reading the bible stories, sitting in that beautiful sanctuary. Could that account for the warm feeling of intimacy with his son he was now experiencing? He had not shared such a moment with Richard for a long time. Wouldn't it be wonderful, he thought if Richard comes out of this if he could become the kind of father his own father was not?

Richard's right hand rested on the bed above the covers. The IV was connected to his left forearm. He took Richard's hand in his. The skin was soft and cool to the touch. "I'm glad to be here," he said out loud.

He was supposed to talk. They were encouraged to talk. He put both of his hands over the boy's hand and held it gently.

"I've got a lot to tell you. You won't believe where I've been. I went to a synagogue. Pretty funny, huh? Your old man going to a synagogue? Don't ask me why I went. Okay, I'm sure you want to know, so I'll tell you. I thought maybe if there is a God, I could ask him to help you out. Not me. It's probably too late for me. Anyway, I'm not important enough to go making a trip to a synagogue for. But I thought it would be worth it for you." He paused. Before today, it had always been difficult to get the words out. Now it was suddenly easy.

"I thought nothing happened. I sat there. I read the Bible. I talked to this little guy who takes care of the place. He was really nice. But I thought none of it did any good. Now I'm not so sure."

He swallowed. "There's something else I want to say. I know I haven't been a good father…everything that's been wrong between us is my fault. Plain and simple.

"What I mean is, I'm the adult. You're the child. Even now, you're still the child. I should have been better. I couldn't accept the idea that you would turn out to be gay. I was afraid for you, afraid for myself. It was up to me to behave better, to understand what you were going through." His throat constricted. He swallowed again. "What I want to say is that it's not going to be the same.

From now on things are going to be different. Better. All I want is for you to forgive me."

He took a deep breath. His throat was as dry as if he'd hiked across the Egyptian desert. He let go of Richard's hand and stood up. Richard's breathing continued as regular as a metronome. He glanced at the monitor, still the insane stick figures marching off the end of a cliff.

He bent over and kissed Richard's forehead, then sat down again. He suddenly felt immensely tired. His neck and shoulders ached. In fact, his body was begging him to lie down and sleep. He held Richard's hand and bowed his head. He heard sounds in the corridor, snatches of conversation. After a while, he raised his head and looked at Richard. He thought he saw his eyelids twitch.

"I saw them move," he said out loud. "I'm sure I did. Come on. Do it again."

Sure enough, there was movement, slight, but perceptible. "Listen. I don't know if you can hear me but save your strength. I'm going out to get somebody."

He hurried out to the nurse's station and persuaded a skeptical nurse to go back to the room with him. When they walked in, Richard's eyes were open.

"This is great," the nurse said. She wrapped one hand around his son's wrist to take his pulse. "Try talking to him. Let's see if we get a reaction."

"Richard. It's me. Dad. How're you doing?"

The boy's eyes were open but they were vacant. There was no response.

"It's all right," she said. "It's not unusual. Coming out of a coma is often very gradual. A little bit at a time. It doesn't happen suddenly like in the movies."

"Does this mean he's coming out of it?"

"Oops. I'm a nurse, not a doctor. Don't quote me. I'm going to let the doctors know right away. They're the ones you have to talk to."

"But it's a good sign, isn't it?"

"You better believe it."

"Richard," he tried again. "It's me, Dad. You're going to get out of this. You hear me? Everything's going to be okay."

His son's eyes suddenly seemed to click closed as rapidly as a camera shutter.

"What happened?"

"I can't tell you. Nobody really knows what's going on inside a comatose patient." She laid Richard's arm back on the bed. "I'll inform the doctors." She left.

Soon Miriam came back. She nodded at Alex and told him that JaMarcus had gone home for a while.

Alex told her what had happened. Not what he had said, just the part about Richard's eyes opening.

"Does it mean anything?"

"According to the nurse, yes. It's a sign he may be coming out of it."

Miriam began to cry.

He moved closer and put his arms around her. She did not pull away. She leaned her head on his chest and allowed him to hold her. For the first time in a very long time, he felt something good had happened.

Chapter 48

Miriam's eyes were closed but tears continued to flow. She could feel her body trembling, could feel Alex's arms holding her in an embrace. It was both comforting, and at the same time, not quite right. She moved away from him.

"I'm sorry. Don't know what got into me."

"Don't be silly," Alex said. "It's quite understandable."

"So what happens now?"

"The nurse said she was getting a doctor. Let's wait and see what they say."

A few minutes later the nurse came back along with a young doctor. Miriam thought he looked familiar but wasn't sure if she'd seen him before.

"Hi," he said. "I'm Doctor Molinari, a resident here." He bent over Richard, felt for his pulse, looked at the monitor. Then he turned to them and asked, "What exactly happened?"

"My son opened his eyes," Alex said. "I was talking to him and his eyes opened."

"Anything else?"

"Then they closed."

The resident had a round face with a small mustache that Miriam thought he'd grown to make him look older, but to her, he still looked like a little boy. He smiled at them. "That's a very good sign. It shows his vitals are good, and that he may possibly be coming around. Of course, it's too soon to tell. I must warn you, that it may also be an anomaly."

"But you think something may be happening?" Miriam asked.

"I can't say any more than what I just told you. Of course, I'll report this, but sorry to say, these cases are unpredictable. We'll keep watching and hope for the best."

After he and the nurse left, Miriam went over to the bed and kissed Richard on his forehead. His skin was smooth and cool. "I think I'll sit here a while, then I'm going home. What about you?"

"I'll do the same," Alex said. "I don't want to go back to work."

Miriam's thoughts were swirling, her mind projecting a future with Richard smiling and telling her about the part he just got in a new play. She knew it was fantasy, but it helped to relax her and she felt the tension in her body gradually abating. After sitting for some time, she felt her eyes begin to close. She fought against it but found herself dozing off, only to awaken again almost immediately.

She got to her feet. "I think I should go. I'm feeling really tired." She picked up her handbag. "I'll see you later, I imagine."

"Yes," Alex said. "Drive safe."

When Miriam got home she decided to have a warm bath, hoping it would help her relax. She stayed in the tub until the water began to get cold. She brushed her hair, dressed in pajamas and a warm robe, and then went downstairs to the den.

She liked this room. The furniture consisted of a couch, a recliner, and a comfortable armchair. There was a glass wall that looked out into the garden. At this time of year, the trees were beginning to lose their leaves, and the shrubs, except for the evergreens, were turning yellow.

Fall was ending, winter would soon arrive, always a kind of sad time of year, but at the same time providing a sense of continuity. She put back the recliner and looked out, glad to be in the comfort of her own home.

After a while she closed her eyes, expecting to drift off. The moments passed, but it didn't happen. Her mind began tumbling from one thought to another, the way it did sometimes when she woke up in the middle of the night and found herself unable to go back to sleep.

Of course, she thought about Richard, her beautiful child. He was no longer a child, but someone who comes out of your womb is somehow always your child. She had never given up hope that he would recover, but now there were signs that he was on that road. She wouldn't allow herself to get excited, but at least she had good cause to be optimistic.

She wished her father were still alive so that he could put his arms around her and tell her everything was going to be okay, the way he did when she once fell and scraped her knees. She didn't have too many memories of him because he died when she was only six years old. What she did remember were the smells she associated with him, tobacco smoke, and a spicy after-shave lotion. And when he hadn't shaved, the rough stubble of his cheeks when he picked her up and kissed her.

He was an accountant and took her to his office one day to show her where he worked. He introduced her to his boss and his secretary, and they made a big fuss over her and told her how pretty she was.

They lived on Eastern Parkway in Brooklyn, not far from the library, the botanical gardens, the Brooklyn Museum, and Prospect Park. He took her to the zoo and gave her a pony ride. He took her to the botanical gardens and to the museum. How nice it would be if he were here now to comfort her and her mother. Sentimental claptrap, of course, but still felt good to think about.

ⲉ⳹ⲟⲉ⳹ⲟ

When she was a bit older she went after school to all the same places, not the pony ride of course. The connection to her father was always there. Her favorite was the library. It was huge and had rooms with welcoming armchairs, where you could sit and read and nobody would bother you. Her mother asked her once why she spent so much time there. "It's such a great place, Mom. I just feel good being there, surrounded by all those wonderful books. I love to just sit there and read."

She was smart enough to get high grades in school, so it was strange that she couldn't make up her mind about what she wanted to do with her life. The guidance counselor gave her a list of colleges where she was sure Miriam could get a scholarship, but to her chagrin, Miriam declined.

"You're making a big mistake," the counselor said. The counselor was Miss McDermott, built like a brick shithouse she'd heard a boy say. A no-nonsense woman who wore too much makeup and a gigantic string of fake pearls.

"Maybe I am," Miriam said. "But I just don't want to spend four more years in school. I want to get into life. I want to get into the world."

She really had no idea of what she meant by that. What she knew was that school was dull and boring so it seemed probable that the world of commerce and action would inevitably be more interesting and exciting. She envisioned herself in a skyscraper looking out over the city while giving orders to an assistant.

"You're making a big mistake, young lady," said Miss McDermott.

She signed up for secretarial school, and after one year, got a job in a law office. It turned out to be even duller than school, and when one of the partners groped her ass one day, she slapped his face and walked out.

From there it was a series of jobs, none of them interesting, which made her finally realize she had indeed made a huge mistake by not going to college. The *life* she'd envisioned had not turned out to be exciting or anything that she had imagined as a teenager.

She had thoughts of perhaps trying to go to college. She was still young, only twenty-one. There was no reason she couldn't do it. It might be tough financially, but she was sure her mother would help.

She was seriously looking into it when she fell in love. The moment their eyes met that day in the Strand bookstore, she felt something. It wasn't quite like Cupid's arrow but there was definitely a spark. This was new to her. She'd been out with guys, had slept with two. The first one was someone she'd known in high school. The second was one she'd met on a blind date. Neither experience had been satisfactory. There'd never been any real excitement, and she was quite sure she hadn't had an orgasm.

That day, the moment their eyes met, Alex dropped his eyes and then quickly looked up again to see that she was still looking. He smiled. Nice smile. She put down the book she'd been holding and walked around the table to where he stood. "Hi," she said. "What are you looking for?"

"I don't know. Something, anything that catches my eye. Why? Do you work here?"

She laughed. "No. I'm just browsing, like you."

"Is that what you call it?"

"What do you mean?"

"Want to go and have coffee or a drink?" he said.

"Are you trying to pick me up?"

"I thought you were trying to pick *me* up?"

"Is that so." She laughed. "Well, maybe I was. Looks like I succeeded." She took his arm. "By the way, my name is Miriam. What's yours?"

∽∾∽

She heard a car pull into the driveway. The side door opened and Alex came into the house. She closed her eyes and pretended to be asleep. She was drained and exhausted and couldn't bear the thought of talking to anyone at this moment. His footsteps took him through the house and eventually to the den. She felt his presence in the doorway and kept her eyes closed. He remained there a while, probably deciding whether to wake her or not, then she heard him go upstairs.

She couldn't hide forever. They would have to talk. But what would she say to him? What would he say to her?

Chapter 49

A few days later the excitement about Richard had receded. Richard had not opened his eyes again, nor had he made any other movements. The doctors were still hopeful, if not optimistic. They were coming to see Richard once more, their interest apparently revived.

His mother was back again, meticulously put together, as usual. A touch of makeup, a simple gray dress with a string of pearls. "I wish there was something I could do," she said.

She sat with them in Richard's room. There wasn't much in the way of conversation. When a visitor was there it inhibited the attempt to talk to Richard and stifled even ordinary comments.

After some time his mother asked if anyone wanted coffee or a cold drink and invited Alex to go with her.

When they were in the corridor, she asked, "How're you and Miriam doing?"

"Not very well. It's like we're all in a state of suspended animation. I don't think about anything but Richard."

In the cafeteria, they ordered coffee and sat at a table. "You haven't done anything else, have you?" she said.

"You mean, about my sister?"

"Yes."

"What do you take me for? I told you. All I care about right now is Richard."

"I was hoping that's what you would say. But I just wanted to hear it."

"Well, now you heard it."

His mother reached out and put her hand over his. "I pray for him every night," she said.

"Thanks," he said, his eyes filling. "He can use all the help he can get."

Chapter 50

For reasons unknown, even to himself, Alex felt compelled to read his father's diary once more. He read what his father had written about Clarice. About the thoughts and the desires.

But what about his mother? Was she one of those women who look away, refusing to acknowledge what they suspect is going on in their own house? He had read about a daughter who had come to her mother with blood running down her leg after a visit from her father. And the mother's response was: "Clean yourself up." He didn't think his mother fit into that category, but he couldn't help wondering how much she knew.

Clarice had begun writing poems after she came out of the hospital that first time. He could not recall a single line but remembered that they contained the names of the planets and the stars. She loved their sound: Uranus…Saturn…Jupiter…Achernar…Antares…Sirius…She would read them to him in her reedy voice that quivered with emotion. She read him other poetry, as well. He remembered one single line because she quoted it so often. It was from William Blake. He was her favorite…Cruelty has a human heart…"Don't you think that's so true?" she would ask him.

He would nod his head not knowing what it meant.

Two days before she died she had called him at school

from Boston where she was in detox. She had asked him to meet her there.

"What for?"

"I need to talk to someone. You're the only one I can talk to."

"I can't! I can't cut classes now. I've got exams. Wait for the weekend. I'll come on the weekend."

"I can't wait."

She had sneaked out and gone to a hotel. What they found in the hotel room was the present he had given her for her eighteenth birthday.

"I hope it brings you good luck," he had written on the card. It was a piece of rock the Hayden Planetarium claimed was from a meteorite that had crashed onto the Earth centuries before. He had seen it in the gift shop on a class expedition to the Planetarium and had made a special trip there on his own to get it for her.

"I'll keep it with me forever," Clarice had said.

He had walked in on Clarice once when she was fifteen. The bathroom door had not been locked and she had just come out of the shower. She was holding a towel, about to dry herself, her arms upraised. In the brief hot moment, he saw everything, particularized, detailed, as if he were examining one of his stamps through a magnifying glass: her breasts were small, pointed, the nipples pink and tender, the curve of her hip silken, the triangle patch curly-damp. His first sight of a live naked woman. He had backed out stammering, apologizing, but that image had reappeared for a long time, exciting him and then making him feel dirty.

Just once he had tried to speak to her.

"Does Daddy go into your room at night?"

"Sometimes."

"What does he do in your room?"

"He comes in to say good night."

"Does he stay long?"

"Sometimes. Sometimes he sits on the bed and talks to me."

"What else?"

"Nothing else."

"Does he…does he…touch you?"

"No-no-no…Daddy loves me…"

She was sobbing loudly, and he took her in his arms to calm her down. "I'm sorry. I didn't mean to get you upset. Forget about it. Forget I said anything."

Chapter 51

When he arrived at the hospital Miriam and Ja-Marcus were standing and watching a doctor who was seated at the side of the bed talking to Richard. Richard's eyes were open.

"Okay, Richard, let's try again. What's your name?"

The pupils of Richard's eyes were dilated, dark blue circles. He was looking at the doctor. It almost seemed as if he were staring at him. He didn't answer.

"Tell me something," the doctor said to Richard. "Do you know where you are?"

Richard looked at him but still didn't speak.

"Listen to me, Richard. I'm a doctor. My name is Joe Hazlitt. You're in a hospital. I want to know if you can hear me. I'm going to ask you a question. If you can hear me, try to blink your eyes. You don't have to speak. Just blink your eyes if you can. Okay?"

He waited. There was no response.

"You said you were going to ask him a question," Alex said.

The doctor turned toward Alex. His head was shaved as smooth as a grapefruit. "That's right. I said that, didn't I?" He turned back to the patient. "Do you know where you are, Richard?"

He waited.

Alex realized he was holding his breath.

There was no response.

"What's going on?" Alex asked. "When did he open his eyes again?"

"About an hour ago," Miriam said. "JaMarcus and I were sitting here and all of a sudden we noticed his eyes were open. We called a nurse and she called the doctor."

"I'm a neurologist," Hazlitt said.

"What do you think?"

"I understand he had his eyes open before. Is that right?"

"Yes. Yesterday."

"It may indicate that he's coming out of the coma. But it's important to understand that there are no guarantees. I've been trying to get a response from him for quite a while now. But I've gotten nothing." He looked at Miriam. "You're his mother?"

She nodded.

"Why don't you try speaking to him? He might respond to you."

Miriam took Richard's hand. "Darling. It's me, Mom. Can you hear me? Say something, sweetheart. Nod your head. Blink. Do anything."

Alex said, "I think I saw something."

"What?"

"His eyelids. Didn't they move a little?"

"I don't think so," the doctor said. "But don't give up. Keep trying." He stood up. "I'll be back later. If anything happens, ask the nurse to page me."

After he left, JaMarcus went close and said, "Hey Richie boy. It's me…Buddy. You hear me? I love you, man. I want you out of here. I want you home with me. You hear? You got to respond, man. You got to respond!"

Richard's eyes remained open but he gave no sign of having heard or understood anything.

"He's going to make it," Alex said. "I know it. This is

just the beginning."

"I think you're right," JaMarcus said.

Miriam leaned over and pressed her lips gently to her son's cheek.

Alex felt something he hadn't felt in a long time. A glimmer of hope for them now. Richard's illness was bringing them closer than they had been in years. There was a sudden yearning in him to confess everything to Miriam. The desire was like a bubble of air, bottled up inside him, moving around trying to find an exit. But he also knew that now was definitely not the time to do it. All it might do is blow everything apart, and create in her, not hysteria, but worse, a fierce rage, something he could not possibly cope with at this time.

Chapter 52

When he got to the office the next morning, Wanda was at her desk with the other women huddled around her. Wanda's eyes were red-rimmed. She'd obviously been crying.

"What is it?" Alex asked.

Ruthie said, "The poor girl. Her mother's been moved into hospice. We told her to go home. How can she work in a situation like that?"

"Absolutely," Alex said. "Wanda, I'm so sorry to hear this. There's no reason for you to be here. Go to your mother. It's where you ought to be."

Wanda patted her eyes with a tissue. "Thank you. I'll come back tomorrow."

"Come back only if you feel like it. We can manage. I'll let Mr. Roth know what's going on."

Two days later, Wanda called Ruthie and told her that her mother had died. She gave her the date, time, and place where the funeral was to be held.

"It's in the middle of the week," Ruthie said. We won't be able to go."

"You can pay a condolence call later. I'll go and represent us."

"Will Mr. Roth let you go?"

"I'm not asking. So don't worry about it."

At lunchtime, he called Wanda from a phone booth.

"The cancer spread into her liver," she told him. "There was no chance of saving her."

"I'm so sorry."

"We never got along. It was one of those mother-daughter personality things. Oil and water. You know. Everything she said got my goat. Everything I did bent her out of shape. But I always loved her. She went through hell for me. And now it's too late."

"Is there anything I can do?" He knew it was an inadequate response but couldn't think of anything else to say.

"I don't think so. I'm not coming to the office tomorrow, either. I have to make arrangements for the funeral. My father can't do it. He's too broken up."

"If you need any help with the funeral arrangements..."

"I can handle it," she said. "But thanks for the offer."

He had been given directions to the funeral home. It was somewhere in Brooklyn. He couldn't seem to help being drawn back to that borough. "You can walk from the station," Wanda had told him. "It's only a few blocks."

It was an incredibly long, seemingly endless ride. The train was a local that stopped at a station every few minutes. The doors would open, people would leave, others would enter, the doors would close, the train would thump-thump along to the next station where the procedure repeated itself.

He had not wanted to go. Who wanted to go to funerals? The death of a parent was difficult, especially one so young—her mother had only been fifty-five. Her family would be there, strangers he didn't know, didn't want to know. But he owed it to her, of course. How could he not go to her mother's funeral?

When he finally got out to the street he took deep breaths, glad of the fresh air.

The funeral home was on a corner lot surrounded by a white picket fence—the kind that should have enclosed

Hansel and Gretel's house. The building was white clapboard done in Southern Plantation style with tall columns bordering a verandah. The shrubs that surrounded the building were trimmed into rectangles, circles, and ovals so tight the leaves formed a solid mass.

He went through double doors and saw the usual faceless men wearing black. He abruptly realized he did not know Wanda's mother's married name. "I'm here for the funeral at eleven."

"The waiting room is that way. The guest book's over here."

He wrote his name, then went into the room where a large number of people were standing and talking in low voices. He looked for Wanda and saw her seated on a love seat. Beside her was her daughter, Judy, whom he recognized from the photograph in Wanda's apartment. In the photograph, there had been little resemblance to Wanda, but seated next to her there was no doubt of their relationship. They were both wearing similar black dresses, the younger with one arm around the shoulders of her mother, whispering something to her. There was something startlingly beautiful in the way they looked together.

He headed towards them when he became aware of a sudden movement across the room. He turned and saw Rudi Emmenthaler. Emmenthaler. What was he doing here? He had turned up at his father's funeral and now he was here as well.

He saw Wanda look up. Their eyes met. At the same time, Rudi was moving through the crowd in his direction. He saw Wanda look at Rudi whose face had turned pink and whose arms were now moving in circles like a swimmer in heavy surf.

He was in their house on the street with the postage stamp lawns and wrought iron gates, brick steps leading to the oval door, and the chimes that clanged three notes when you pressed the bell. They were in the living room and he was showing them the diary and the letters. And Rudi's wife was the woman his father had had the baby with and she would not tell him how to find her daughter—his sister. "Leave her alone!" she said. "F," the diary, of course, Rudi's wife, looking worn and ill, wearing a turban to hide the loss of hair from chemo.

Now Wanda looked from Rudi to him and back again, puzzled. She did not know that Rudi knew him or that he knew Rudi. How could she? He could see that she was trying to work it out.

He had already done it. The knowledge coalesced in his brain the way elements come together in the fusion of an atom. Only in his case, there was no explosion. Instead, he felt anesthetized, trapped in one of those dreams where everything moves in slow motion.

Rudi was now in front of him. "She begged you to leave us alone. And you follow her, even to the grave. Can't you leave us in peace?"

"Francesca is Wanda's mother," Alex said.

"Of course. Why are you here? Who told you about the funeral?"

"Wanda asked me to come."

"Wanda? What do you have to do with my daughter?"

She stood next to them now. "What's going on?" she whispered. "Everyone is looking at you."

"I'm sorry," Alex said.

"This is my father."

"We already met."

"Where would that be?"

"It's a long story. I'll explain another time."

She tugged his hand. "Come. I want you to meet Judy."

He felt Rudi's eyes following him as she led him to her daughter who surprised him with a hug and kiss.

"Mom has told me so much about you."

He wondered how much. "She's told me about you, too."

"She says you're so nice to work for."

"And she's nice to work with."

There were other words spoken, other introductions. He was barely aware of them. He was trying to deal with the information that had suddenly been jammed into his unwilling brain. He was woozy. His eyes glazed over. His legs were shaking. He had to take a series of deep breaths to keep from falling.

The funeral went ahead. Wanda invited him to ride to the cemetery in her limo with her daughter and Rudi. It was impossible to refuse, so he agreed. He spent the entire time staring out the window, watching the traffic on the parkway. No one spoke.

The husband, daughter, and granddaughter stood together as the casket was lowered into the ground. Alex stayed well back, trying to be as inconspicuous as possible.

They were going back to Rudi's house after the cemetery. He told them he could not go with them, he had to be at the hospital. Wanda's eyes were asking questions but she said only that they would speak later.

"Yes," he said. "I'll call you later."

Chapter 53

He walked back toward the subway station in a state of confusion. The revelation had hit him, not like a spear piercing his brain, but more like someone slamming a fist into his guts. His original idea had been to attend the funeral as a mark of respect and then go to the hospital to see Richard. But right now he needed to think. He needed time and space. So he went home. Once there, he headed straight down to the basement without turning on the lights. It was interesting, wasn't it, that he so often found the basement a place of comfort? Just like his father? He sat in the dark and let his thoughts rattle back and forth like dice on a crap table.

The basement was damp and smelled of mildew. The telephone rang. He listened to it ring four times then quit. The answering machine in the bedroom must have come on. He wondered if Miriam had changed the announcement or if it was still his voice.

He took out his pouch and pipe. There was a faint light coming in from a narrow window but he did not need it to fill the pipe. He had done it what, a thousand times, ten thousand times? He scratched a match and puffed, drawing the smoke into his mouth, pulling it rapidly in anticipation of the familiar pleasure. But this time the smoke was rancid, and he blew it out, spitting with disgust. He threw the pipe, and heard it hit the tile floor. He was glad. He hoped the pipe was broken. Somehow, breaking something that belonged to him seemed like a good thing.

My God, what was he going to do? He would have to tell Wanda, but how could he? What would that knowledge do to her? For that matter, what was it doing to him?

He couldn't sit still. He went up the stairs and out into the garden. He opened the shed, picked out a four-pound hammer, a pair of pliers, wire, and a half dozen wooden stakes which he had set aside some time ago when he had noticed there were places where the fencing needed repair. He took off his jacket, folded it neatly, and laid it on the ground. He put on a pair of work gloves, propped up a section of fence that was leaning, drove two stakes around the rotting post making it firm again. He then secured the fence to the restored post with the wire, twisting the wire tightly with the pliers. He stood back and checked his work. It was a job his father would have belittled, finding fault with some part of it. But now he realized for the first time that his father's continual criticism of him did not make his father feel good. That coldness, that inability to show affection for his son was a demonstration of a crippling flaw. He ought to feel sorry for the old man instead of hating him.

He could see the old man as he used to be—denim work shirt buttoned to the collar, chino pants, thick-soled black shoes. Underneath that working-class exterior had been a person he had never known or understood. And after reading and rereading the diary, he wasn't any closer to understanding him. He wondered how much of his father's blood was in his.

He did another section of the fence, this one more difficult. He could feel sweat in his eyes, running off his nose. This was what he needed, thought prevention. He paused a minute and observed the colors of the leaves. They fell as he watched, slowly at first, then gradually increasing in velocity. Suddenly, they let go all at once, swarming over him in a torrent of copper and gold. He could feel their dryness as they brushed across his face. It was hard to breathe. He felt a moment of panic. He covered his nose and mouth with his hands, shut his eyes, and waited for it to end. After a while he took his hands away and opened his eyes.

Then he saw that nothing had actually happened. The leaves were still on the trees.

He took off the gloves, put his jacket back on, and walked around to the front of the house. He stood on the sidewalk, looked up and down the street, and as usual saw no people, just well cared for houses and neat landscaping. It wasn't a bad neighborhood. Safe streets, a lot of people working hard, struggling to get ahead, which meant what? A bigger TV, a luxury car? He had been one of them. All his life he had been one of that pale-faced amorphous mass, hanging on by his fingernails.

But that was changed now. Hiding wouldn't work any-more. Facts had to be faced. Decisions had to be made. Wanda was, of course, Angelina. Wanda was his sister. Technically, his half-sister but that made no difference. Not wanting to, he remembered her naked...her breasts and belly shining with musk oil. The things they had done together. He thought he was going to be sick. He opened his mouth and sucked air. She had to be told. She deserved to be told. He wondered how she would react. What would she say? What would she do?

An automobile drove down the street and pulled up to the curb in front of him. His mother's black Camry. She got out of the car and came over to him. She wore a per-fume that smelled like roses.

"I was on my way home and saw you on the sidewalk. What are you doing here? Is everything all right?"

"Oh sure. I had to go to a funeral. Someone's mother from work. So I decided to come home instead of going back to work. Everything's fine. How are you?"

"Not very well," she said.

"Why? What's the matter?"

"Perhaps you forgot. I'm a widow. I'm not used to being alone. Sometimes I want to crawl into a hole and hide. I want to escape from all reality. A friend of mine who's a widow tells me I'm going through a 'healing' process. I hope she's right, that it's all worth it. I don't see the end. I feel like I'm hurting all the time."

This was something new. His mother was actually talking to him. He realized that he'd been so self-absorbed, that he hadn't given any thought to her. She'd lost her husband. She had a right to grieve. On an impulse, he put his arms around her. She didn't pull away.

"You know what I do?" she said. "I keep my friend's phone number written down all over the house. Even though I know it by heart I need to see it so that I can call her anytime I feel like it. Did you ever hear of anything so silly?"

"Never."

She looked into his eyes as if she had just noticed something. "Are you sure you're all right?"

"I'm fine, Mom. Richard's improving. I think he's going to be okay."

"I'm glad," she said. "You take care now."

She got back in the car and drove away.

Chapter 54

He sat at the side of the bed and watched his son. He was intensely aware of the steady breathing, the tubes, the monitor lines moving endlessly, the occasional clicking sounds, and the murmurs from the people moving in the corridor. But he also was aware that he no longer felt as if he existed in a void, a limbo of abandoned souls. After a while, he went out of the room.

At the end of one corridor, there was a phone booth. He called Wanda.

"I'm at the hospital."

"Any change?"

"Not today. Not yet." He hesitated. "I have something important to tell you."

"I know."

"You know?"

"My father told me. He's very upset."

"I was hoping to tell you in person, not on the phone. He told you everything?"

"He didn't want to, but I kept after him."

"So…what now? How do you feel? You must be very upset yourself."

"Of course I am. It was quite a surprise."

"Surprise? That's all? You're just surprised? It doesn't bother you that you were fucking your brother?"

"Half brother."

"Same difference."

"What do you want me to say?"

"I thought at least you'd be shocked."

"I'm not."

"You mean it actually doesn't matter to you that you were committing incest?"

Her voice became hard. "I don't see it that way. For one thing, I didn't know it at the time. OK? And you're not a real brother. It's not like we grew up together."

Alex sighed. "I'm sorry. I'm not trying to beat you up. But I am beating myself up. I'm more than upset about it. I can't help it. It bothers the shit out of me. I've been trying to figure things out ever since the funeral. And I'm getting nowhere."

"What exactly are you trying to figure out?"

"I don't know. My life?"

"There's something else that's bothering me. Your mother wrote a letter to my father. She said she was going to name the baby, Angelina. If she named the baby, Angelina, and you're the baby, where did Wanda come from?"

She laughed. "I hated the name, Angelina. I went to school one day and told everyone my name was Wanda. That's what it's been ever since."

Chapter 55

Miriam woke up one morning and decided it might be a good idea to pay a visit to her business. She hadn't been to the store in a long time, too long. She'd had good cause, of course. She hadn't been there because her son was more important than anything else. But now things had changed and for the better. For the first time, she could allow herself to feel optimistic about Richard. He'd made strides, opening his eyes, seeming to comprehend. It now seemed that it would only be a matter of time before he fully recovered. At least she could tell herself that without thinking that she was only fooling herself.

She was there at 9 before the store opened at 10. She unlocked the front door, switched off the alarm, turned on the lights, and looked around. What she saw made her smile. Everything was as it should have been. The store was sparkling clean and inviting. The displays were set out properly, attracting the eye.

She went to her desk and looked for the records of bank deposits, and daily receipts. What she saw made her smile again. The business had been doing quite well, averaging almost a thousand dollars a day in gross receipts. Effie, her manager had been doing an outstanding job. She trusted her, had to trust her because where cash was involved there was always the chance of stealing.

Miriam looked to see what had been ordered, received,

and what bills had to be paid. Writing checks was her responsibility alone. She saw that a few invoices were past due and resolved that after she had gone over them with Effie, she would get that done.

Effie came in at a quarter of ten. She was wearing a gray pantsuit with a pearl-gray blouse. She always looked professional. When she saw Miriam she rushed over and gave her a hug and a big smile. "This is so great. I didn't expect to see you here."

"I decided it was time to check up on you."

"Absolutely. Don't blame you."

"You know I'm kidding. The store looks really good. And from what I see, we've been doing pretty well."

"It's been fabulous. We practically have no time to sit down. People are traveling like crazy these days. They love what we have for them. But I have to tell you, we need to do a lot of re-ordering."

"Fine, let's go over everything and decide what to do. How's Sylvia?"

"Good. She'll be here any minute."

"How has it been working out with the part-timers? Have they been holding their end up?"

"No problems to speak of."

"Well, all good news. That's nice to hear."

Effie put her handbag down behind the front counter. She turned and said, "I hope you don't mind my asking, but how are things going with your son?"

"Of course, I don't mind. I'm happy to tell you there's been some improvement. That's why I felt able to come here today. The doctors say they think he's coming out of his coma. They won't predict anything, but they really seem to be optimistic. I know I am. So yes, things are finally looking up in that department."

When Sylvia came in there were more hugs of welcome. Miriam sat down with Effie and went over the list

of items to be re-ordered. While they were working, customers began coming into the store, enough of them so that
they had to stop what they were doing and wait on them.

Miriam found herself enjoying this so much. It was
agreeable to answer questions and make sales. Doing the
actual physical and mental work, having contact with people, wrapping up the sale, packaging the merchandise, processing the credit card, or taking the cash and putting it
into the cash register, all these simple and menial tasks
were giving her the most pleasure she'd had in a long time.
God! How she missed a normal life. If only the rest of her
days could be as normal and as pleasurable as this. When
she'd first opened the store her marriage had been good
and her son had been healthy and she herself had been
healthy. So much taken for granted. She decided to stay
through their lunch hour and then go back to the hospital.

Chapter 56

Alex had been working sporadically for weeks. Some days he would work a few hours. Other days he would not go in at all. He had told Roth this was the way it had to be as long as his son needed him.

He was still in a state of shock about Wanda. He had no idea what, if anything, he was going to do about it. This morning he decided to work, thinking it would be a good way to escape the insanity of his personal life. He went in early. He bought the Times out of habit but didn't read it. What was the point?

He went to his desk and began to go through the stack of paper on it. The details never changed—collections, processing of orders, credit checks, faxes, files, photocopies. He was glad to see them. It was reassuring to be able to do what he knew he did well.

Luis, the foreman, and the men showed up, which reminded him that the question of unionization was still not resolved. Then Ruthie came in, followed by Estelle and Gloria. He did not expect to see Wanda so soon after the funeral, but she arrived shortly after the others.

There were remarks to Wanda about how sorry they were about her mother. They asked him about Richard. He told them about the improvement but didn't go into detail. He and Wanda looked at each other but did not speak. Then they all got down to work.

Mr. Roth came in about ten o'clock and immediately took Alex into his office. "Am I glad to see you," he said. "We are buried here. Absolutely buried."

"I'll get it cleaned up," Alex said. "I'll stay late."

"Good. It's been murder with you out so much. Listen, you've been working for me a long time. I feel like we have a relationship, not just boss and employee. And I know you've got a lot of trouble in your life, but the world goes on Alex. Life goes on. I've got a business to run."

"I understand."

"So I hope we won't have any more of your not being here."

"I'll try my best."

"Great," Roth said. "I know you will. And if I didn't say it before, I am really glad you're back."

"I'm glad to be back," Alex said.

Seated at his desk he knew he wasn't. Glad to be back. He had said it, but it had been an automatic response. And saying they had a "relationship" was a total lie. That was Roth the Salesman using his selling technique to get him to work harder.

He worked steadily until he heard the factory shut down for the lunch hour. Ruthie and Estelle left together. He asked Wanda, "How do you feel about lunch? Gloria'll hold the fort."

Wanda shrugged. Outside, the sky was clear, the sun warm for the end of October. "Are you hungry?" he asked.

"No."

"Neither am I."

The sidewalks were filled with lunch hour people. There were wagons on every corner selling souvlaki, kosher hot dogs, falafel, gourmet salads, chocolate chip cookies, Häagen-Dazs. The streets rumbled with automobiles and trucks. They walked a few blocks without talking.

"How about we just get a hot dog?"

"Fine with me."

He got two hot dogs with mustard and sauerkraut, and they stood near the food cart and ate them.

"Let's walk," Alex said. They went along Mott. "Chinatown. Remember the last time we were here?"

"We met Richard."

"Yeah. That was a total disaster." They walked another block. And Alex said, "I don't know what to say to you."

"Then don't say anything."

"I can't help it. I'm all torn up. Conflicted."

"I don't know why you keep agonizing over this. What's done is done. Just let it go." They headed back. A crowd had gathered around the subway entrance on Canal. It spilled over into the street further obstructing traffic. There were a few police cars with emergency lights flashing and two EMS ambulances.

There was nothing to see except a mass of people pressing forward and the spinning colored lights on the official vehicles. Alex asked one of the cops standing around what happened.

"Somebody on the tracks. Got hit by the train."

"Suicide?"

The cop shrugged. "Who knows? Whatever. It's all over now."

There was movement in the crowd. They made a space for two men carrying a body bag on a stretcher. The men shoved the stretcher into an ambulance, slammed the doors, got into the front, and drove away. The crowd began to break up.

After they returned Alex worked steadily for several hours. Then he stood up and walked into Roth's office.

"I'm quitting."

Roth looked at him, eyes widening behind his glasses. "What?"

"I'll stay as long as you want, within reason, until you find somebody."

"What are you talking about? What do you mean, you're quitting?"

He had never noticed before how much Roth resembled a squirrel, with that pointed little face. He would not have been surprised to see his nose twitch. "That's right."

"But why?"

He sat in the chair opposite Roth's desk. "I'm forty-nine," he said. "Next stop, fifty."

"What's the big deal? I'm almost there myself. I don't even think about it."

"I do. It means more than half my life is over."

"It happens to everybody if they're lucky enough to make it to fifty."

"I only know I don't want to keep doing this."

"Then what are you going to do to make a living? Be realistic. What's out there for you?"

He did not want to tell Roth he had once been a teacher, that it was something he might be able to do again. He knew what a derisive response that would get.

"I don't know. I'll find something."

Ross shook his head. "I think you're having what they call a mid-life crisis."

"I'd say you're absolutely right."

"So what are you going to do about it?"

"I already told you." Alex stood up. "I'm quitting."

Chapter 57

On the way to the hospital, he stopped at a Duane-Reade for toothpaste and while he was there, bought a notebook.

Miriam and JaMarcus were at the hospital. They greeted each other. Then continued the routine that they had established in which the three of them took turns talking to Richard, singing to him, reading the newspaper. When they took a break they played the TV. Richard's eyes were open often now, and occasionally there was an encouraging response like the blinking of eyes or a squeeze of the hand.

After a couple of hours, Alex said he was tired and going to head home. Miriam said she would go as well. JaMarcus usually stayed later.

He had come without a car. This had occurred several times now with Miriam driving the two of them. This also had become somewhat of a routine. The awkwardness had faded away, along with the tension. A truce had been not been formally declared but it was understood to exist. They were now more like two old friends who had hurt each other once but had since reconciled. When they came back from the hospital Miriam made tea and they sat together for a while.

"I quit my job," Alex said.

Miriam put her cup down, her eyes widening. "Really?

What made you do that?"

"I guess I finally realized I hated it. Hated what I was doing. It was a dead end. I was going nowhere. Life is short. All the clichés of a midlife crisis, probably."

"You know what?" Miriam said. "Good for you."

It wasn't until almost midnight that he was alone in Richard's old bedroom. He thought of how intrigued he had once been catching glimpses of himself in Richard, genes reproducing themselves in telltale strokes: pulling his ear, the way he brushed his hair back with his left hand, moving his lips when he concentrated. He remembered his sense of helplessness when it became clear to him that Richard would never see any of those things in a son of his own. Now it didn't seem to matter.

He emptied the bag from Duane-Reade on the desk. He took the toothpaste into the bathroom then returned to the desk and sat down. He stared at the notebook he had just bought.

It was almost as if his father had commanded him to do this, the way he used to order him to mow the lawn, and not just mow it, do it right. But now he wasn't resentful. In fact, he felt a kind of pleasure in what he was doing.

His father would come out of the house towards the end of the job, stand in the driveway in the long-sleeved white shirt he wore every day, and show him the parts of the lawn that needed to be done over. He didn't point with a forefinger, he made a fist out of his thick hand and pointed with his thumb. Then he would always add, "Don't forget to rake up the clippings".

That's what he was doing now...raking up the clippings.

He remembered the maple chairs in the kitchen. When one of the rungs on a chair loosened, his father would take it down to the basement and reglue it. He went down once to see how it was done, but his father didn't want him there. *This ain't for you. Go play your clarinet.* His father would return the restored chair to the kitchen and sit at the table, his face flushed, pulling his lips in and out as if he were biting like a toothless crone. It was a long time before Alex realized with a shock that he moved his own lips the same way.

He pulled open the drawer of the desk and looked to see what was in there. There were a couple of pencils, a ballpoint pen, a compass, and a six-inch ruler made of red plastic. The points of the pencils were gone.

He took the pencils and went downstairs to the kitchen. He used a kitchen knife to make points on both pencils then went back up the stairs. Miriam's door was closed. No light was visible around its edges. The house was quiet. He was glad of the stillness. He switched off the hall light and stood for a moment in the dark.

He went back into the bedroom. He sat at the desk and held the pencils in his hand. He stared at the white rectangle on the cover of the book. It was identical to the black and white school notebooks they'd been manufacturing forever…identical to the one that was on the night table.

He brought roses to Miriam the first time they went out. "That's so romantic," she said. "Are you a romantic?" "No," he replied. "But I think I'd like to be."

With his left hand he turned back the cover and exposed the blank first page. The lines were ruled in blue ink.

She had been a skinny girl when they married, all bones and angles. On a weekend in the country, they had gone for a walk and come across a huge meadow that seemed endless. The grass reached their hips. They rolled around in it like children. They lay on their backs and held hands and looked up at the sky. They made love in the grass, scratchy on their naked bodies. They were alone on the earth, it was all theirs. It was one of the best days of his life.

He put one pencil in the drawer and held the other in his hand.

He had tried to pay his debt to Rudi. He had called him. "I apologize for what I've done to you. I meant you no harm."

"But harm you did. You poisoned my Francesca the last days of her life."

"I meant nobody any harm."

"I am sorry for you. I am sorry for Wanda. I am sorry for my Francie, to die so young. She was an unusual woman. When she went with Max she was only nineteen years old. She did not want to marry but wanted a child. What attracted her to your father she did not tell me, just that it was him she chose."

"Do you think he loved her?"

"He did. It was Max who told me to help. And when me and Francie married, he told me he was glad that Francie would have a husband and the baby would have a father. I will always be grateful to him. My life with Francie was a blessing I never expected.

"He cared about his whole family. He had love in him but he was a closed-up man. He could not show it. He never got over his little girl, Clarice."

He turned one more page. The memories were coming at him furiously now…vivid as graffiti.

He placed his left hand flat on the outer page of the book. He began to write:

I don't know why I bought this book.

I want to write down what I feel. Maybe it will help.

One thing I do know…I am not my father's son.

He read the last words he had written, then underlined one word so that it read,

One thing I do know…I am <u>not</u> my father's son.

He stopped and pulled open another drawer. There was a book in it. He took it out to see what it was. It was a bible.

He recognized it as the bible Mr. Natterman, the man from the synagogue, had given him. He opened it and began to read:

In the beginning God created the heaven and the earth...

Did the words mean anything? Would he ever be able to figure it all out?

There was a noise somewhere. He raised his head, shifted, so his ear could catch the sound.

He clearly heard the distinctive voice of Mr. Natterman saying, "Maybe, perhaps."

രാഗ്ദ

About the Author

Robert Boris Riskin has been writing fiction for most of his adult life. He studied playwriting at the University of Michigan but switched to fiction shortly thereafter. While trying to become a writer he worked at a variety of jobs from dishwasher to busboy to factory work to owning retail stores selling discounted clothing to high-fashion women.

He has published stories in The New Yorker and numerous literary magazines. He has also published three mystery novels featuring a retired English teacher and Shakespeare maven who solves crimes while quoting Shakespeare.

A Brooklyn native, he has traveled the world, even lived in France for two years while studying at the Sorbonne.

But New York is where his heart is. He now lives in Sag Harbor, where the bay and the ocean are nearby and the air is filled with creativity.

Please visit his website:
www.robertborisriskin.com